ECUMENISM...
FREE CHURCH DILEMMA

ECUMENISM...
FREE CHURCH DILEMMA

Robert G. Torbet

THE JUDSON PRESS, Valley Forge

ECUMENISM . . .
FREE CHURCH DILEMMA

PREFACE

IN A DAY WHEN CHRISTIANS of all branches of the church are seeking each other in fuller understanding, more effective witness, and joint action in mission, the number of books concerning aspects of the ecumenical movement is increasing to the point where justification is needed when one adds still another volume to the extensive body of literature now in existence.

The purpose of this small volume is to explore the Free Church principles as they relate to the quest for Christian unity. It has long appeared to the writer that those who are committed to the Free Church concept need to reassess their position with a view to determining what is basic and essential and what can be relinquished in the interest of a united Christian witness. The dilemma of the Free Churches is how they may relate to a movement for the recovery of a unity which was broken, in part at least, by their own dissent. They protested against the authoritarianism and institutional rigidity of the medieval church which, in their minds, had jeopardized its authentic witness by its identification with the state and its accommodation to a sub-Christian culture.

This volume may also help those who belong to the more institutionalized state-church background to understand what is of primary importance to free churchmen as the two traditions meet in ecumenical encounter and dialogue. American Christians, in particular, who enjoy a heritage of religious liberty, need to distinguish between the theological and political foundations of this heritage. While there are, to be sure, points of similarity between the Free Church principles and political democracy, there are risks of assuming that the spiritual roots of the Free Church position are identical with the eighteenth century foundations of American democracy, which were based more largely upon a philosophy of natural rights than upon a Christian understanding of man's response to the gospel. To the clarification of such issues, this book is dedicated with the earnest hope that the achievement of better understanding will contribute, on the one hand, to an intensified effort on the part of the Free Churches to draw closer to other Christians and, on the other hand, to a fuller appreciation of the Free Churches by Christians of other traditions.

ROBERT G. TORBET

CONTENTS

Chapter 1

THE DILEMMA OF THE
FREE CHURCHES INTRODUCED

THIS IS A BOOK about "Free Churches" and how they conceive of Christian unity. It is pertinent to the widespread discussions of how Christians can find each other across the barriers of denomination, class distinction, economic status, and racial background. The mounting interest in dialogue among Protestants, Orthodox Catholics, and Roman Catholics has stimulated in nearly every denomination an exploration of its history, its reason for existence, and its relationship to other Christians. That this is a healthy ferment cannot be denied. Yet, it confronts all Christians with the dilemma of choosing between loyalty to a denomination which in itself represents only a part of the whole church and loyalty to the ultimate reality for which Christ came into the world—the new humanity in which all are truly one in him. It is the tension between the actual and the ideal, between the partial and the whole, between the accidents of history and the purpose of God.

This tension or dilemma is especially difficult for those churches which trace their origin to a radical protest against the compromise and evils they saw in the Christendom of medieval Europe. In their search for a viable renewal of the Christian witness in a culture-dominated Catholicism, these reformers rejected the union between the church and the state, between Christ and culture. They sought the restoration of primitive Christianity with its radical devotion to Jesus Christ and his way of life. They believed that they were called to a radical obedience—to serve God rather than men, to be faithful to the Christian ethic even if this meant disobeying the state. These radical reformers withdrew from the state church in protest against its corrupting compromise with the secular order, and formed congregations of "believers" who voluntarily covenanted to walk together under the discipline of Christ. It was in this sense that they were "Free Churches"—seeking freedom from a compromising connection with the state and from an institutional church which they believed had allowed the purity of primitive Christianity to become distorted by religious ceremonies, dogmas of church councils, the authoritarianism of politically minded bishops, and the biblical illiteracy of the laity.

Among the forerunners of these Free Churches were groups within the Roman Catholic Church such as the Waldensians of the twelfth century, their counterparts the Franciscans who shared their spirit in many respects without breaking with the institutional church, and the Lollards who arose in fourteenth-century England as followers of John Wyclif. When the Protestant Reformation gathered up this protest into a widespread movement of reform in the sixteenth century, the Lutherans and some of the Calvinists and Swiss and Dutch Reformed maintained a connection with the state; but others broke with the state and maintained a separate existence as self-governing churches voluntarily supported by their members. Among these were the Anabaptists of Switzerland, Germany, and Holland. Their successors are known today as Mennonites after Menno Simons, a Dutch priest who became one of their greatest leaders. Others included the Huguenots of France, who were followers of Calvin's teaching; the Separating Puritans or Independents of England, who were forerunners of present-day Congregationalists; the Baptists; and the Society of Friends, who emerged out of English Puritanism in the seventeenth century. Presbyterians were forced into separation from the state during their unsuccessful struggle with Parliament (1642-1649) to establish a Presbyterian state church in place of the Anglican (Episcopalian) established church. When Methodism arose in the eighteenth century under the leadership of John Wesley, it remained within the Church of England until after his death, whereupon it proliferated into several Methodist bodies which remained separate from the state.

The Christianity which was transplanted to the English Colonies in America in the seventeenth century was destined to emerge as Free Churches in the new Republic created following the American Revolution. The Constitution of the United States, which took effect in 1789, included separation of church and state as a protection to religious liberty in a pluralistic society. Accordingly, all Christian churches in the United States are in fact free churches, although only some of them trace their heritage to the historic Free Churches which arose as a part of the reform movement that began in medieval Europe and culminated in the Protestant Reformation of the sixteenth and seventeenth centuries.

It is in this context that we undertake an exploration of how the Free Churches, which had rejected the unity of Christendom in favor of the separation of church and state, conceived of Christian unity. In Chapters Two, Three, and Four, we endeavor to trace the emergence of the Free Church tradition, to delineate the essential of the Free Church witness, and to describe the Free Church understanding of Chris-

tian unity. Chapters Five and Six are intended to be illustrative of the Free Church reaction to the quest for the
healing of the divisions that were the product of the Protestant
Reformation. The Baptists and Disciples of Christ have been
selected, partly because they are best known to the writer and
partly because they are alike in many respects yet different
in their approach to Christian unity. Both share a restorationist zeal to recover primitive Christianity with its emphasis
upon personal commitment to discipleship, symbolized in
their mutual rejection of infant baptism in favor of baptism
of believers only, in their congregational polity, and in their
adherence to the principle of the separation of church and
state. They differ, however, in the fact that the Disciples are
committed to being a uniting church whereas the Baptists
tend to sacrifice unity to their emphasis upon personal freedom
and congregational autonomy. The final chapter seeks an
answer to a number of questions which reflect the dilemma
of the Free Churches. Can the Free Churches commit themselves fully to church union without sacrificing fundamental
principles? If so, on what basis? If not, what is the future of
the ecumenical movement, since such a large segment of
Protestantism is today composed of the Free Churches and
of Christians who are sympathetic with their tendency to
distrust institutional Christianity and visible corporate unity?

The dilemma of the Free Churches is how to participate in
the current ecumenical movement which calls for a commitment to Christian unity that includes communions identified
with the state, when the traditional stance of the Free
Churches is to reject the concept of *corpus Christianum*
(Christendom) and ecclesiastical formalism. Some may argue
that the dilemma is past because we live in a post-Christen-
dom era and in a time when the institutional aspects of the
church are being widely challenged. However, the institutional life of the church is not without support in the ecu-

menical movement, especially when one sees it in the full scope of Protestant-Orthodox-Roman Catholic participation. Accordingly, the dilemma persists for the Free Churches if they are to take their place in the present era of dialogue and growing unity.

Chapter 2

THE FREE CHURCH TRADITION

THE FREE CHURCH TRADITION by its very name implies a protest against any infringement upon the essential liberty of the people of God to be obedient to the lordship of Jesus Christ. It is an aspect of Christianity which was only a minority expression in medieval times, but which received a new lease on life during the Protestant Reformation, first on the continent in the Anabaptist movement and then in England in the emergence of Puritan separatism (or congregationalism). Fostered by a propitious set of circumstances in the eighteenth and nineteenth centuries in both Britain and America, the Free Churches gained an increasing measure of recognition and acceptance. Their success was due in part to the proliferation of Protestantism, creating a pluralism which made it difficult for any single denomination to win full support of the state as the established religion. It was due also to the enlightened spirit of tolerance fostered by the deists whose leadership in the political revolutions of England and America was aligned with the Free Churches in their common struggle for representative government and the principle of voluntaryism in religion.

Perhaps nowhere in the world has the Free Church tradition achieved such general acceptance as in the United States. Favored by the political liberalism of the deists and nurtured by the frontier spirit of a young and vigorous pioneer society, evangelical Christianity won the struggle for religious liberty and the separation of church and state. Yet, at the same time, there was no rejection of religion by the state. Instead, the allegiance to basic Christian affirmations and principles became a part of the American way of life. Statesmen, politicians, literary men, and educators all assumed that the noble experiment in which they were engaged was an endeavor to achieve a free nation under God which might properly be called "Christian."

The twentieth century has witnessed a decline in the impact and influence of the Free Churches in Britain. In the United States the basic assumption of a free church in a free society is still accepted but not uncritically. There are those who are apprehensive of a new religious pluralism in which the Roman Catholic and Jewish faiths are claiming increasing attention, thereby threatening the nineteenth century assumption that this is a Protestant America. Even within the Free Churches the perennial spirit of renewal, which is inherent within this tradition, is causing the more earnest Christians to ask whether the churches have not accommodated the gospel to the secular spirit and interests to the extent that their message and life has become an acculturated rather than a pure form of Christianity.

Still another factor contributing to the changed status of the Free Churches is the modern ecumenical movement. Beginning in 1910 in an international conference on world missions, it has grown into even broader dimensions now involving dialogue between the World Council of Churches and the Roman Catholic Church. The concept of seeking Christian unity through councils of churches has given way, in the thinking of many, to a search for more visible union in Christ in fulfillment of Christ's prayer for the church (John 17:20-23). Because the British Free Churches and the Church of England share in the ecumenical venture, the stance of the former has become for many less pressing and significant. In the United States, where all churches enjoy equal status in the state, and where an increasing number are in conversation with each other and are involved as members of ecumenical councils, and, in some cases, are participants in consultations for union, the Free Churches are obliged to reexamine their presuppositions at those points where they have differed historically with the national churches; namely, apostolicity vested in the historic episcopate, creedal and liturgical uniformity, and centralization of authority over the congregations.

The need for reappraisal is of major importance for two reasons. On the one hand, Christians of all traditions are becoming increasingly aware of the unhappy effects of their divisions upon the effectiveness of their witness to the Good News that God is forming a New Humanity bound in Christian love. On the other hand, these same Christians are aware of the deep convictions on which agreement has not yet been reached and without which any move toward ultimate unity may be superficial and lacking in integrity. Consequently, the search for visible oneness in Christ must be made on the basis not of indifferentism, but of an honest and open evaluation of the respective traditions in the light of the purpose of God as revealed in the reconciling ministry of Jesus Christ which he has entrusted to his followers.

BIBLICAL ROOTS OF THE FREE CHURCH VIEW

Some find the roots of the Free Church principles in the

New Testament emphasis upon the gospel of grace in place of the legalists' system of merits. Others, looking backward, see them rooted in the interpretation of the Bible by Calvin and earlier Fathers of the church who found no hierarchy, no gulf between clergy and laity, no apostolic claims to supreme authority, no support for the view that monarchial episcopacy was essential to the existence of the church. They found, instead, that the whole church was the Body of Christ and that "the ministry was the gift of Christ to men to proclaim the Gospel and to serve, not to rule over, the Church."[1]

Gunnar Westin, one-time church historian at Uppsala University, argues that "the primitive Christian assembly was a free church in that it had no relationship, subordinate or co-ordinate, with any constituted authority or the state."[2] While it might be debated whether or not this was an accident of history rather than a theologically determined position, there is some cogency in Westin's equation of the apostle Paul's formula that faith comes by means of preaching the Word (Romans 10:17) with an essential freedom of proclamation.

Ernst Troeltsch, the nineteenth-century sociological analyst of the church, described the message of Jesus as a proclamation of the kingdom of God, out of which inevitably emerged a social order. Inherent within this message were two revolutionary principles: absolute individualism and absolute universalism, both requiring each other. The early church, he believed, had a low esteem of existing institutions and refused to submit to them. It was essentially a new community at odds with the world and earnestly convinced that it must maintain independence from secular institutions. Gradually,

[1] Henry Townsend, *The Claims of the Free Churches* (London: Hodder and Stoughton Limited, 1949), pp. 18-19, 67.

[2] Gunnar Westin, *The Free Church Through the Ages,* trans. Virgil A. Olson (Nashville: The Broadman Press, 1958), p. 2.

however, the church came to see that it was destined to remain in the world because the eschatological hope of Christ's imminent return had faded. Convinced that it could not ignore secular institutions, the church therefore tried to utilize them for its own purposes. As a consequence, "the old charismatic gifts and free offering of service were logically transformed into a hierarchical sacerdotal system."[3]

The Christian movement closed ranks and regarded the rest of life as the "world." Laymen, eager for heaven, withdrew from society into a monastic life. Primitive Christianity yielded to an early form of Catholicism with its priesthood, episcopate, canon, tradition, and sacramental ideas. In fact, the church turned from the synagogue pattern with its lay leadership to the temple pattern with its priestly leadership, Yet, as Troeltsch reminds us, the primitive ideal of the gospel was not dead. "It lived on in ideas and in institutions, although it had certainly become greatly changed in the process."[4]

ORIGIN AND MEANING OF FREE CHURCH CONCEPT

There are those, like Westin, who see spokesmen for the Free Church viewpoint in the protesting groups which arose after A.D. 180, when the monarchial episcopate emerged and the process of centralizing the local congregations in synods began. Among these were the Marcionites, the Montanists, the Novatians, and the Donatists, all of whom protested against sacerdotalism and the institutionalization of Christianity. In later centuries this position was upheld in varying degrees by the Waldensians in Italy, the Lollards in England, and the reformers of the sixteenth century.

The fundamental protest was against the medieval concept of the essential unity of church and culture (*corpus Christi-*

[3] Ernst Troeltsch, *The Social Teachings of the Christian Churches* (New York: The Macmillan Company, 1949), Vol. I, p. 99.

[4] *Ibid.*, p. 161.

anum) in which the church was no longer opposed to the secular order, but was a spiritual sphere destined by God to be superior to the temporal sphere. The church, as the purveyor of God's grace, was the instrument for the redemption of society and for its incorporation into the will (or kingdom) of God. The protesting groups already named arose from time to time alongside of the institutional church to protest against this view, which they regarded as a compromise with a sinful world-order. The protesters stood for a literal and uncompromising application of the ethic of Jesus which would be directed to the conquest of self and to the achievement of brotherly love. They regarded the church as a close-knit community of committed disciples who avoided any contaminating involvement in the social forms of the world. The church was to be in fact a company of Christ's disciples who embraced his ideals of poverty, suffering, and holiness. It was opposed to the state; indeed, it regarded the secular order as antithetical to the attainment of the supernatural aims of life. Union with God, they believed, could only be achieved by self-denial and asceticism. The church was in truth a community of converted individuals striving for perfection, exclusive in its membership, and universal only in its eschatological hope, not in any visible form here on earth.

These views were expressed in medieval times by Waldensians, Franciscans, Lollards, and the Hussites of Bohemia. While some were more critical of the Catholic hierarchy than others, all were generally agreed in several respects. First, they were opposed to the materialized institutionalism of the church expressed in its great wealth, in its sacramental system, and in its ecclesiastical offices and courts. Second, they identified the law of Jesus with the law of nature, imposing a literal application of his teachings on their followers. Third, they manifested a mystical piety in their style of life. Fourth, they were enamored with an apocalyptic prophecy which pointed to the fulfillment of history in the coming kingdom of Christ.[5]

Franklin H. Littell, a present-day church historian, describes the radical Christian protest against ecclesiastical authoritarianism in the sixteenth century as having taken three forms. The first was the most radical or "Maccabean" Christianity, which comprised a kind of pre-socialist revolutionism. It was typified by men like Thomas Muntzer and Jan of Leyden. The second was composed of the spiritualizers, like Sebastian Franck (1499-1543), Caspar Schwenkfeld (1489-1561), Anne Hutchinson (1591-1643), and James Naylor (1618-1680), who emphasized the immediacy of God's revelation to the individual through the Holy Spirit. External forms of religion were abandoned in favor of an emphasis upon the inner reality of faith and devotion to God. A third and more moderate form of sixteenth-century radicalism was what Littell calls "Integral Christianity." Its exponents—men like Conrad Grebel, Balthasar Hubmaier, Menno Simons, and John Robinson—found the true church in visible disciplined covenantal communities of those who, in response to the grace of God, had entered into a covenant with God.[6]

One important aspect of this radical obedience was its stress upon personal freedom and responsibility. Peter Riedemann, foremost theologian and hymn writer among the Hutterites, taught that: "The conscience is free, and the Christian is responsible only to God; therefore, the magistrate has no dominion over faith, nor can it molest the conscience of mankind."[7]

[5] The foregoing analysis is based largely on Troeltsch, *op. cit.*, Vol. I, pp. 333-378.

[6] Franklin H. Littell, *The Free Church* (Boston: Starr King Press, 1957), pp. 26-42.

[7] Westin, *op. cit.*, p. 110, based upon Peter Riedemann, *Rechenschaft unserer Religion* (1543).

Littell affirms that the basic essential of the Free Church which determines its style and emphasis is "the conviction that the terms of reference for the church are not fixed by a hierarchy or by a Sanhedrin, but by the process of talking up a consensus among the whole believing people."[8] This concept of freedom to discover the will of God should not be regarded as an ultimate and individual freedom; for it involves accepting the yoke of Christ, not autonomy. Moreover, the present-day tendency to define the separation of church and state as church versus state is in error because it assumes incorrectly that we begin a discussion of the Free Church with the political issue instead of with the mission of the church in which service that is pleasing to God is voluntary and uncoerced.[9]

Properly understood, the Free Church view begins with a radical break from the regional territorial pattern that characterized both medieval Christendom and many of the Protestant denominations that followed the Reformation. It takes a primitivist view of church history, relying upon the New Testament as the norm for the faith and life of the church. Accordingly, apostolicity means being true to the message of the apostles, not maintaining continuity with the apostles in the episcopacy. The Free Church view seeks to keep in tension the "gathered" (*ecclesia*) and the "scattered" (*diaspora*) aspects of its life. The church is conceived of not so much as a pattern but as a mission. The general priesthood of all members is stressed and expressed in a congregational structure of church life. The Free Churches present an alternative to an order established by the prince or town council in "voluntary covenants openly arrived at and willingly sustained." Church government is based upon consensus (derived from the prin-

[8] Franklin H. Littell, "The Historical Free Church Defined," in *Brethren Life and Thought*, Vol. 9, No. 4 (Autumn, 1964), p. 78.

[9] *Ibid.*, pp. 78-82.

ciple suggested in Acts 15:28: "It has seemed good to the Holy Spirit and to us"). The Free Church concept at its best conceives of men of Christian conviction and ability bringing to town councils and other structures of society "a new style of public and political action."[10]

REFORMATION AND FREE CHURCH TRADITION

The Reformers of the sixteenth century, in varying degrees, took steps to renew or cleanse the church of its worldliness.[11] Essentially, they focused their attack upon the papacy and bishops who they felt were self-seekers, politically ambitious, and lacking in true devotion to Christ. Martin Luther saw a basic theological issue in the scholastic (Aristotelian) emphasis upon the form of the sacraments to the point of distorting the biblical view of salvation by faith alone. He presented a new concept of the church according to which its essence lies in the Word, the sacrament, and the ministry in a strictly spiritual sphere of influence. He did not deny the universalism of the church, but was willing to see it expressed through territorial churches rather than through Rome whose spirit he regarded as anti-Christ. Luther also distinguished between the temporal and spiritual elements in society without separating them. The economic life and the molding of society by Christian ideals he left to the state whose policies might be influenced by those with Christian principles.

John Calvin stressed knowledge of God as the fundamental base for salvation. It was to be a knowledge achieved through the Scriptures, illumined by the Holy Spirit, which leads one to Christ the source of our salvation. Like Luther, Calvin did not reject the concept of the unity of the spiritual and tem-

[10] *Ibid.*, pp. 83-88.

[11] The author is indebted in this section principally to Troeltsch, *op. cit.*, Vol. II, pp. 465-576, 581-625, 705-729.

poral spheres of society. But he laid more stress on the natural law than did Luther, believing that it could be used in the creation of the Holy Community. The *corpus Christianum* was for Calvin the unified society, built up by the influence of the sacred and the secular. The Christian community had a responsibility to mold life in the secular society.

The Brethren (or Anabaptists) arose, under the stimulus of the Reformers' loyalty to the idea of the priesthood of believers and a personal religion of conviction, to form communities of the truly converted on a basis of voluntary membership. They rejected infant baptism and its implications of an all-inclusive, non-ethical basis of church membership, because of its wide separation from confirmation when personal decision could be expected. They insisted upon church discipline and the authority to excommunicate. They were impatient with the course of the Protestant Reformation which allowed continuance of a compulsory state church, and gave rise to a new theological dogmatism, but which had not broken with secularism. They opposed the idea of the institutional church and an ecclesiastical civilization (or *corpus Christianum*).

The Anabaptists began at Zurich and spread to Augsburg, Moravia, Strassburg, and later to Friesland and the New Netherlands. The Peasants' Revolt emerged not from them but from the Hussite and Taborite ideas that the absolute law of God should be enforced in the natural realm. The Mennonites, gathered by Menno Simons in the Netherlands after a period of severe persecution, stressed keeping themselves separate from all non-Baptist Christians. According to Professor George H. Williams of Harvard, they constituted "a radical break from the existing institutions and theologies in the interrelated drives to restore primitive Christianity, to reconstruct, and to sublimate." He saw their emphasis upon believer's baptism as "the symbol and the constitutive principle of the church reconceived, not as a *corpus christianum,* but as a people in covenant, a scattered remnant ever anew being assembled by God's Spirit and his Word."[12]

In England the reformation took a more moderate course. The teachings of Luther, Calvin, and the Anabaptists spread in varying degrees to the Church of England, arousing a response within its membership among those who sought its renewal. These were known as Puritans because they sought to restore the church to its pristine purity on the grounds of the Scriptures and according to the practice of primitive Christianity. The sources of their objection in the sixteenth century were the diocesan episcopacy, which they regarded as lacking in dedication to its spiritual ministry, ceremonial practices for which they found no precedent in the New Testament, and the lack of strict discipline of the members. Some, not able to tolerate the imperfections which they found in the established church, separated themselves from it, forming independent congregations which recognized no other authority than Jesus Christ himself. They were known as separating Puritans in contrast to the non-separating Puritans who continued to recognize the Church of England as their fostering-mother, while working to bring it into line with the presbyterial pattern set by the reformers at Geneva. Both groups were Calvinistic in theology. They differed principally over the way by which to purify the Church of its compromise with the world.

Out of English Puritanism emerged the Baptist movement. Like the continental Anabaptists, Baptists were small groups of earnest Christians, living apart from "the world," claiming complete civil and religious freedom. They rejected infant baptism and embraced adult baptism as the outward symbol

[12] George H. Williams, *The Radical Reformation* (Philadelphia: The Westminster Press, 1962), p. 846. Copyright by W. L. Jenkins, used by permission.

of voluntary membership in a covenant relationship. Unlike the Anabaptists, who stressed freedom of the will, they were Calvinists in their emphasis upon the divine initiative in man's salvation.

In time other Calvinists, like the Baptists, challenged the validity of the state-church system with its acculturated religion and sought to replace it by a voluntary church independent of state control. Like the Baptists also, they adopted a puritanical strictness of life, but fell short of the Baptist ideal by retaining infant baptism. This English Puritan separatism was congregational in church government, having broken with the Church of England. One of its leading clergymen, Pastor John Robinson, when taking leave of William Brewster and the Pilgrims who were enroute for America, illustrated certain Free Church principles: belief in the guidance of the Spirit, faith in private judgment, a sense of expectancy, and a willingness to experiment. He urged them to remember an article of their Church Covenant, "that you be ready to receive whatever Truth shall be made known to you from the written Word of God." He also said: "I am verily persuaded, the Lord has more Truth yet to break forth out of His holy Word."[13]

The English Revolution of 1642-1649 not only brought Puritanism to power but also precipitated its fragmentation. The Separatists (or Independents) found it necessary to coexist with other Christians by a policy of mutual toleration "if they were to battle successfully against the Presbyterian drive for domination."[14] This independent theory of coexistence came to life in Cromwell's Establishment. The Committee of Triers, created in 1654 to pass on the fitness of parish priest nominees,

[13] Daniel Neal, *History of the Puritans* (New York: Harper & Row, Publishers, 1844), Vol. I, pp. 269-270.
[14] James Fulton Maclear, "The Birth of the Free Church Tradition," in *Church History*, Vol. 26, No. 2 (June, 1957), p. 115.

was composed of thirty-three clergymen and ten laymen—primarily Congregationalists and Presbyterians, with several prominent Baptists. Unity was reinforced among the sects by close military association as they discovered that they had a common goal of preventing the Presbyterians from establishing a national church. Some chose dynamic revolutionary action to achieve a new social order through such groups as the Fifth Monarchy Men, the Levelers, and the Diggers, all of whom upheld religious freedom, civil liberty, and equality.

When the Cromwell era came to an end and the monarchy was restored, Puritanism declined, religious variety remained dominant, and the major dissenting bodies, with later additions, became permanent factors in British history. Independency was concerned "not with amalgamating with a dominant part, but with bringing the state to abandon its exclusive support of the advocates of episcopacy."[15]

Many regard the Act of Uniformity of 1662, instigated by irate Anglican bishops against their Puritan critics, as the real beginning of nonconformity. Some 2,000 Presbyterian clergymen and 200 Congregationalists were ejected and so swelled the number of Separatists, Baptists, and others already outside the Established Church.[16] By 1689, the dissenters won a degree of religious toleration after the peaceful revolution in which the Stuart monarch James II was replaced by William and Mary of Orange, who were to be constitutional monarchs.

The Free Church principles inspired the founding fathers of America. In 1786 the Legislature of Virginia passed a famous statute which became what Ernest Payne of England calls "the accepted view of most Free Churchmen in all parts of the world":

[15] *Ibid.*, p. 128.

[16] Ernest A. Payne, *The Free Church Tradition in the Life of England* (London: SCM Press Ltd., 1944), p. 45.

We, the General Assembly, do enact, That no man shall be compelled to frequent or support any religious worship, place or ministry, whatsoever, nor shall he be enforced, restrained, molested, or burthened in his body or goods, nor shall otherwise suffer, on account of his religious opinions or belief; but that all men shall be free to profess, and by argument to maintain, their opinions in matters of religion and that the same shall in no wise diminish, enlarge, or affect their civil capacities.[17]

In a very real sense, the foundations of modern democracy are to be found in the Free Church principles inherent in English Puritanism. Horton Davies has pointed out that men learned the art of Christian government in the congregational meetings of Independents (or Congregationalists) and Baptists, and the class meetings of the Methodists. "The religious sectarians," he writes, "were a seed plot of democracy, because in their autonomous churches every member shared in the responsibility for ruling the affairs of the church, and had experienced the cut and thrust of ecclesiastical debate."[18]

THE FREE CHURCH MOVEMENT AFTER 1689

Westin says that "The new free church [i.e. Puritan congregationalism] was far removed from the narrow view of culture and circumscribed society characteristic of the Anabaptists of the sixteenth century."[19] In both England and the American colonies the Free Churches became a significant factor in political trends as well as in the religious life of the two peoples. After 1689, they enjoyed remarkable growth in England. Nearly one thousand chapels were built, the ma-

[17] Ernest A. Payne, *The Free Churches and the State* (London: The Carey Kingsgate Press, Ltd., 1952), p. 7. Anson Phelps Stokes, *Church and State in the U.S.* (New York: Harper & Row, Publishers, 1950), Vol. I, pp. 393-394.

[18] Horton Davies, *The English Free Churches* (London: Oxford University Press, 1952), pp. 8, 70.

[19] Westin, *op. cit.*, p. 224.

jority of which were Presbyterian, with the Baptists and Congregationalists following in second and third place. From 1727 to 1828 they made continuous efforts to repeal the Corporation and Test Acts through the organization of Presbyterian, Congregational, and Baptist ministers of London into "Three Denominations" (1727). In 1732, a committee was set up known as the "Dissenting Deputies," which brought together laymen as well as ministers from all churches within ten miles of London "to defend and extend the civil rights of Dissenters."[20]

During the era of Napoleon and the Industrial Revolution, the expansion of the Free Churches was aided by several factors: (1) the sympathetic attitude of nonconformists to the American and French Revolutions, (2) the evangelical revivals which won for them new converts, (3) their active participation in a new philanthropy which supported the creation of educational institutions and measures for social reform, (4) the impetus of a Protestant missionary movement begun near the close of the eighteenth century in which Baptists, Methodists, and Congregationalists were in the vanguard.[21]

During the reign of Queen Victoria in the nineteenth century, the Free Churches were cut off from the main currents of secular life because of the legal disabilities placed upon them as nonconformists. Accordingly, they sought equality of privilege with the Church of England and also unity among themselves. In 1813 a General Union of Baptist Ministers and Churches was formed, followed by the organization of a Congregationalist Union in 1831. For several years, beginning in 1834, nonconformists pressed for abolition of church rates. In 1844 they formed the British Anti-State Church Association in their struggle for full civil and religious rights. In this

[20] Payne, *The Free Church Tradition . . .* , p. 63.
[21] *Ibid.*, pp. 89-90.

period their cause was advanced by great preachers such as Rowland Hill of London, Robert Hall of Bristol, R. W. Dale of Birmingham, Alexander McLaren of Manchester, C. M. Birrell of Liverpool, and Charles Haddon Spurgeon of London. But among literary people, there were only two who treated contemporary nonconformity with respect and sympathy—Elizabeth Gaskell and George Eliot.

After 1870, a number of developments began to modify the character of the Free Churches. They were becoming more middle class, and by 1871 nonconformists were admitted to the universities. In 1885 Mansfield College, a Free Church institution, was established at Oxford. The strict dogmas of their Puritan heritage were slackening under the impact of the prevailing liberal climate in theological thought, a trend which was vigorously opposed by Spurgeon from the Baptist pulpit in London. Meanwhile, nonconformists continued their struggle over burial liabilities and payment of church rates.

The period from 1900 to 1960 was one of uncertainty. On the one hand, Free Churches formed world organizations in their respective communions, among which were the Baptist World Alliance (1905) and the World Convention of the Churches of Christ (1930). The National Free Church Council, which had been organized in 1892, was succeeded in 1939 by the Federal Council of Evangelical Free Churches. Relations between the Anglicans and the Free Churches improved following the first World War. In 1920 the Anglican Bishops, meeting at Lambeth Palace, issued the historic "Appeal to All Christian People." Although this invitation to unity was not accepted, both groups entered upon an era of ecumenical good will.[22] This rapprochement was due to a number of factors: their common stand against secularism, their growing sensitivity to the ill effects of division in mission fields, the

[22] *Ibid.,* pp. 134-136.

fact that an increasing number of Free Church ministers shared with the Anglicans a common university background, and the influence of the ecumenical movement.[23]

On the other hand, the Free Churches experienced in this period "acute anxiety" in the face of new problems. A "new theology" was emerging which some regarded as a socialist version of the historic Christian faith. There were constant demands from intellectuals for an accommodation to the new science. Gradually there emerged a combination of a right-wing orthodoxy in doctrine with a left-wing approach to social problems. Spokesmen for this position included Sir Edwyn Hoskins and Professor C. H. Dodd of Cambridge and Scott Lidgett, John Clifford, and Silvester Horne—leading social crusaders.[24]

In the United States during this same period, the Free Church position was so generally accepted in the major Protestant denominations, with the exception of the Episcopalians and Lutherans, that it was all but taken for granted as an integral part of the American religious scene. The separation of church and state was guaranteed by the Federal Constitution. The principle of religious liberty was upheld in the courts. The emphasis upon personal religious response to the gospel was deeply woven into American Protestantism. The social activism characteristic of the British Free Churches, especially the Methodists, took hold among American Christians in the social gospel movement with equal vigor.

Yet, since about 1925, the Free Churches have been declining. Though more perceptibly in Britain than the United States, there are signs in both countries of the waning influence and strength of the movement. Observers in Britain note a decline in church attendance and a lessening of impact on

[23] Davies, *op. cit.*, p. 191.
[24] *Ibid.*, pp. 185-187.

society at a time when the Anglican influence has increased.[25] Although Free Church bodies have become more centralized, they are experiencing a growing sense of uncertainty about their future. Does the course for the future lie in the direction of vigorous denominational emphasis or in the direction of eventual reunion with the Church of England? Are the issues which brought the Free Churches into being still a relevant reason for them to maintain an independent church life? At the very time when a careful study of these questions is needed, a decay of the church meeting, in which Baptists and Congregationalists traditionally handled such issues, and of the class meeting in Methodism, has left these bodies bereft of strong local centers of discussion and decision. As a consequence, there is in many cases a serious gap between the viewpoint of the leadership and of the membership of these church bodies with respect to the course to be pursued.

Westin offers several reasons for the disunity and confusion which has arisen in the Free Churches on both continents. The first is the fact that the struggle for religious freedom, which had held the Free Church movement together in its early days, has been won. The second is that confusion prevails regarding the choice of new objectives. The third is that there has been a cultural leveling process between free churchmen and Anglicans which has created a new openness and fellowship. A fourth reason is that the self-consciousness of the Free Churches has been diminished since the First World War by the impact of the ecumenical movement. A fifth reason is that theological dissension has arisen among the Free Churches as they have had to take a position regarding the claims of the natural sciences, rationalistic philosophy, and the historical-critical study of the Bible. A sixth reason

[25] An example is to be found in Payne, *The Free Church Tradition* . . . , p. 138.

may be found in the preoccupation of segments of the American Free Churches with the "social gospel," which has drawn them into considerations and presuppositions beyond their traditional position. Finally, denominational rivalry among the Free Churches has led to serious difficulties on mission fields, resulting in pressures from the "younger churches" and mission boards of the parent bodies for greater unity among Christians.[26]

EVALUATION OF THE FREE CHURCH TRADITION

Whether the reasons given for the present status of the Free Churches are valid or not, it is urgent that their position be reexamined in the light of new developments in church and state. The ecumenical movement has made it necessary for every denomination to reevaluate its historic position and reason for existence. Moreover, the ever-widening involvement of the state in the total life of human beings in our increasingly complex and fast-growing world population prompts all churches to reconsider their relation to governmental agencies in the face of human problems too vast for any single denomination or combination of denominations to solve alone.

Any reevaluation should begin with the recognition of a number of significant contributions made by the Free Churches. First and perhaps most important is the fact that "their recognition of the primacy of the Gospel over the Church, of revelation over its institutional expressions, has given them an elasticity and flexibility rarely evidenced in Catholic structures of Church organization."[27] In this regard, Ernest Payne asserts that the genuine spiritual life of the Free Churches is capable of creating new forms. This life is the product of a determined endeavor to relate religion to per-

[26] Westin, *op. cit.*, pp. 297-362.
[27] Davies, *op. cit.*, pp. 199-200.

sonal commitment, and a belief in the church as a "gathered
community" which is free from restraints of a uniform liturgy,
of binding creeds, of a priestly succession, and of a particular
form of church order.[28]

Closely related to this contribution is their influence upon
political self-government. Franklin Littell describes it in these
words:

> Yet in the sense that they rejected external political or ecclesiastical
> compulsions, and to the degree that they developed patterns of dis-
> cussion and decision which could be extended to secular voluntary
> associations, they have made major contributions to the theory and
> practice of self-government. . . .[29]

While the Free Churches' emphases upon voluntary societies,
decision by consensus, and personal freedom of conscience
are not as popular today in the highly organized patterns of
modern urban life as they once were, the values which they
have placed on the individual's worth in society provide a
significant legacy to be preserved in an age of conformity.

Less tangible to appraise is the contribution of the Free
Churches to Christian unity. This is so because they have been
less prone to seek visible forms of union, fearing that institutional structures will stifle the life of the Spirit. Professor
Williams of Harvard Divinity School describes the ecumenical
outlook among the sixteenth-century radicals or nonconformists as a "sectarian ecumenicity." It was "a combination
of the sense of the imminence of the Kingdom of God, the
experience of the universality of the work of the Holy Spirit,
the impatience with the territorial particularization of the
Reformation, and the overwhelming conviction as to the actuality of the New Covenant."[30] The ecumenical hope of

[28] Payne, *The Free Church Tradition* . . . , pp. 143-145.
[29] Littell, *The Free Church*, p. 43.
[30] Williams, *op. cit.*, p. 815.

Anabaptists, in particular, lay in their confidence in the ultimate unity of the true church of Christ, and in the hope that
fresh illumination would lead disputants to oneness of mind
and heart. They regarded Catholics and Protestants, no less
than Jews, Turks, and pagans, as the object of their evangelistic
mission. They believed that Christ's death was an atonement
for all people. The fullness of the church, however, is known
only to God and therefore is invisible to men. The visible
church, for Anabaptists, is only an approximation of the pure
"bride of Christ" and is to be found only in local congregations of committed disciples.[31]

Such particularity, exclusivism, and independency have
marked Puritan Congregationalism as well as the Baptist
churches which have emerged from it. Although Baptists of
the seventeenth century reflected a concern for the unity of
the church and often referred to their fellow Christians of
other denominations as brothers in Christ, there was inherent
in their stance a sectarian point of view. For them, the norm
of the true church was to be found in primitive Christianity.
Its most telling mark, they believed, was the covenanting
community of the committed, gathered by the direct work of
the Holy Spirit. The external sign of this community was
believer's baptism, which became the safeguard to a "pure
church" in which each member, without coercion, had responded in faith and obedience to Christ as Lord. While
some, like John Bunyan, refused to allow this act to divide
them from other Christians, baptism did serve to separate
Baptists from other Christians and has continued to do so in
many quarters of this communion to the present day.

The Free Church witness to the primacy of personal response to God's call to a life of obedience and suffering, if
need be, has, as we have seen, made its impact upon other

---

[31] *Ibid.,* pp. 829, 832-833, 839-843.

communions. Indeed, the current trend among many pedo-baptists to restudy the meaning of believer's baptism in the "I-Thou" encounter between God and man has deepened the conviction of many Baptists of the importance of their witness. They have been loath, therefore, to enter into mergers which might in any way threaten this witness. Those Baptists who react warmly to the ecumenical movement seek various ways to preserve their conviction regarding the church as a gathered fellowship without becoming sectarian. By an open membership policy, in which their congregations admit Christians from other communions (which baptize infants) on the basis of their profession of faith without rebaptism, they seek to prevent their view of the church from becoming a barrier to wider Christian fellowship. But, in general, Baptists and other free churchmen who hold similar convictions do not easily think of church union with pedobaptists as a live ecumenical option. Those who do are at the present time a minority committed to find a way to more visible unity on the basis of a fresh approach to the Scriptures in the light of new biblical and theological insights.

Chapter 3

ESSENTIALS OF THE
FREE CHURCH WITNESS

IN OUR DAY when the Free Churches are declining in membership and influence and when many are saying that the Free Church concept of Christianity is outmoded, it is essential for free churchmen to take stock of what precisely is the essence of their position. A careful evaluation of the answer to this question can in large measure determine what, if anything, should be preserved of a point of view which has exerted a significant influence in the history of Christianity. A survey of the development of the Free Church position will reveal what is essential to it.

Free churchmen have looked to the primitive church for the spirit and emphasis upon freedom in Christ which has been their ideal. For them, the basic unit of the New Testament church was the community of faith gathered by the Holy Spirit. It was not an institution, but God's people. This concept, they believed, derived from the Old Testament's central theme of God's covenant with Israel. The authority of this "gathered church" and of its prototype, the gathered synagogue of Israel, is for them the Spirit of Christ in the congregation.[1]

As early as the second century after Christ, Irenaeus wrote, "Where the Spirit of God is, there is the church and every kind of grace."[2] It is the Holy Spirit who establishes and sustains the fellowship which Christians can have with God and with one another. A present-day free churchman has summarized this emphasis in these words:

> It is the Spirit that guides us to the Scriptures; that assures us that Jesus is both Lord and Christ, who works to bind us who are strangers together in church fellowship; and who makes us members one of another.[3]

The unity of the Spirit was the source of the New Testament church's catholicity. To be sure, there was no rigid uniformity of organization nor any single pattern of clerical authority. There were many congregations, varied in structure and leadership. But they never regarded themselves as totally independent of each other. Each congregation had a genuine sense of being part of the Body of Christ and of sharing his mission to the world. In a very real sense, therefore, the gathered companies of believers manifested the church universal without any loss of their adequacy to witness. It has been rightly pointed out that "Congregationalism, except when it seeks complete local autonomy, is not the opposite of catholicity. In the New Testament the two go hand in hand."[4]

[1] Harry H. Kruener, "A Baptist Theology of Church Order," in *Great Themes of Theology*, Lynn Leavenworth, ed. (Valley Forge: The Judson Press, 1958), pp. 154-155.

[2] Irenaeus *Against Heresies*, Bk. III, Chap. 24. 1, in *The Ante-Nicene Fathers*, Alexander Roberts and James Donaldson, eds. (American Reprint of the Edinburgh Edition of 1885; Grand Rapids: Wm. B. Eerdmans Publishing Co., 1950), Vol. I, p. 458.

[3] Robert T. Handy, *Members One of Another* (Valley Forge: The Judson Press, 1959), p. 34.

[4] Kruener, *op. cit.*, pp. 157-158.

The same basic principle was advanced in the fourteenth century by John Wyclif, a precursor of the Protestant Reformation. His spiritual concept of the church led him to insist that man's personal relation with God is paramount and that the Bible is the final court of appeal. He put it succinctly in his theological treatise, the *Trialogus,* when he laid down the principle: "Where the Bible and the Church do not agree, we must obey the Bible; and, where the conscience and human authority are in conflict, we must follow conscience."[5]

John Hooper, Bishop of Gloucester and Worcester in the sixteenth century, was the exponent of a less pronounced but definite spirit of nonconformity which was part of his Puritanism. He remained within the established church, but subordinated ecclesiastical authority to the Word of God. In 1550 he wrote:

> I believe that the people of God, who are the very true church of God, have a certain doctrine, that never was, is, or hereafter shall be, violated by time or any man's authority. This doctrine only and solely is comprehended in the sacred and holy Bible.[6]

Like Calvin, he claimed that two marks of the true church of Christ are "the true preaching of God's word and right use of the sacraments."[7]

Henry Barrowe and Robert Browne were nonconformists of the sectarian variety. They contended for a free preaching of the gospel, a simple administration of the sacraments, and a proper discipline of members. Believing that the Church of England was corrupt, the nonconforming Puritans, under Browne's leadership, set up separatist meetings, concerned for "reformation without tarrying for any." It was from these

[5] Philip Schaff, *History of the Christian Church* (Grand Rapids: Wm. B. Eerdmans Publishing Co., 1949), Vol. VI, p. 323.

[6] *Writings of Dr. John Hooper . . .* (Philadelphia: Presbyterian Board of Publication, 1842), p. 200.

[7] *Ibid.,* p. 214.

Independents that English Puritanism was to draw its powers.[8]

It has been observed that their dissent was "not a revolt from churchmanship, but a new kind of churchmanship." Their withdrawal from the Church of England was a protest against its accommodation to the world. They sought to restore the visible church to New Testament standards by keeping its membership as nearly identical as possible with the invisible church, and its polity in line with the intention of Christ. The Independents conceived of the church as a "mutual confederation" or "solemn agreement" of its members. The covenant into which they entered was "at once a mutual compact and an implicit creed."[9] Browne, it will be recalled, defined the church as "a companie or number of believers, which by a willing covenant made with their God, are under the government of God and Christ, and keepe his Lawes in one holie communion."[10]

Professor Jordan of Harvard traces the Independents' doctrine of private judgment and their claim of liberty of conscience from interference of civil or ecclesiastical power to Calvinistic "belief in the immanence of God and in the actuality of private revelation." They performed, he believes, "a noteworthy service to the cause of religious toleration when they urged that the kingdom of God is spiritual and that the power and weight of the Word are the only possible means for the advancement of the cause of religion."[11]

[8] John T. Wilkinson, *1662 . . . and After: Three Centuries of English Nonconformity* (London: The Epworth Press, 1962), p. 5.

[9] John W. Grant, *Free Churchmanship in England 1870-1940* (London: Independent Press, Ltd., n.d.), pp. 1, 3, 19, 20.

[10] Robert Browne, *A Book Which Sheweth the Life and Manners of All True Christians,* in *The Writings of Robert Hammond and Robert Browne,* Albert Peel and Leland Carson, eds. (London: George Allen and Unwin, Ltd., 1953), p. 227.

[11] W. K. Jordan, *The Development of Religious Toleration in England* (Cambridge: Harvard University Press, 1932), Vol. I, pp. 251-252, 291.

Baptists, who constituted a part of the English Independent movement, took a further step to restore the pristine purity of the church. They rejected baptism of infants in favor of believer's baptism "to ensure discipline and the showing forth of the Kingdom in the church."[12] The Kingdom, they believed, becomes visible in the life and witness of the church through a disciplined congregation. In a very real sense, Baptists believed that the "local congregation provided a focal point for life in the Spirit."[13] It was in the intimate personal relationships of the covenanting community that the priesthood of the believers might be most fully realized. This value, Professor Maring claims, "has contributed . . . much to the enlargement of freedom, both civil and religious."[14]

Baptists were divided on baptism in its relation to church membership. John Bunyan was typical of those who made the church covenant rather than baptism the basis of membership. Without minimizing his conviction that a church should baptize only believers, he refused to let believer's baptism become a bar to communion for mature Christians who had been baptized in infancy. He held to an open membership policy. Hanserd Knollys, a London pastor, represented closed membership, combining "the Congregationalist doctrine of the gathered church with the Anglican conception of the Church as the totality of baptized Christians." He and his followers rejected the church covenant as a basis for membership in favor of believer's baptism. This led eventually to an individualism in Baptist churches unknown among Congregationalists.[15]

[12] Charles R. Andrews, "Christ and Man's Hope," in Leavenworth, *op. cit.*, p. 200.

[13] Norman H. Maring, "Some Thoughts on Baptist Polity," in *Review and Expositor*, Vol. 52, No. 4 (October, 1955), p. 451.

[14] *Ibid.*, p. 453.

[15] Grant, *op. cit.*, pp. 45-46.

The Baptist understanding of the church contributed a threefold solution to what Professor Emil Brunner has called "the unsolved problem of the Reformation": how imperfect earthly churches can be the instrument of God's purpose. First, they held that local congregations should reproduce as nearly as possible the life of faith, obedience, and fellowship; to this end, they rejected infant baptism and insisted on believer's baptism. Second, they acknowledged the primacy of the universal church, which is represented by each local congregation since each has all the necessary powers of the gospel to function for the whole church in a specific place. Third, they devised associations and conventions to express the interdependence of local congregations.[16]

Baptists made a further contribution to the Free Church idea by opposing what Professor Jordan calls the doctrine of exclusive truth with a "subjective relativism" which opened up wide vistas of freedom. For them, "conscience is the organ of an inner light which comes from God."[17] Leonard Busher, the seventeenth-century Baptist prophet of freedom, emphasized, "that God has given to every man the capacities for attaining a saving faith and that every man must find truth in his own fashion and in his own time."[18] He taught that "the spiritual sword of the Word in the hands of Christ's ministers will be competent to destroy all error."[19] It was Roger Williams (1604?-1683) who defended religious liberty on the grounds of liberty of conscience rather than expedient grounds of religious toleration, and who taught, "The Church possesses

[16] Norman H. Maring and Winthrop S. Hudson, *A Baptist Manual of Polity and Practice* (Valley Forge: The Judson Press, 1963), p. 36.

[17] F. F. Powicke, *Henry Barrow, Separatist,* p. 214; cited in Jordan, *op. cit.,* Vol. II, p. 261.

[18] Jordan, *op. cit.,* p. 286.

[19] Leonard Busher, *Religion Peace; or, a Plea for Liberty of Conscience,* p. 55, cited in Jordan, *op. cit.,* Vol. II, p. 294.

spiritual remedies with which it can maintain its own purity, and beyond that it cannot go."[20]

There were inherent risks in this spirit of independency and personal freedom. Always there was the temptation to insure the presence of the Holy Spirit by a proper apostolic succession of ministers or local churches. There was a tendency to repudiate almost completely the institutional conception of Christianity. In the words of W. K. Jordan, "The Bible was viewed as having an inner meaning which was revealed only by the illumination of men's spirits by the Holy Spirit after conversion."[21]

During the struggle between Crown and Parliament in the 1640's the English Independents made great gains with the encouragement of Oliver Cromwell, who was sympathetic with their position. Meantime, the moderate Presbyterians sought to gather the scattered elements of English Puritanism within a broad Calvinistic framework. Their plan for a national church after the pattern of Geneva was no more acceptable to the Independents than had been the Anglican Church. When Presbyterianism, defeated in its effort to establish itself, began to wane in influence in the 1650's, Richard Baxter, a Presbyterian minister with ecumenical leanings, set out to effect an ecclesiastical association of churches in his county of Worcestershire which would embrace independency. He envisioned a communion which would permit complete freedom of disagreement in matters that did not concern the simple fundamentals of faith. These fundamentals he had reduced to the Apostles' Creed, the Lord's Prayer, and the Decalogue. By 1656 associations were either formed or projected under his leadership in sixteen counties. The only

[20] Jordan, *op. cit.*, Vol. III, p. 501, based on *The Bloudy Tenent of Persecution for Cause of Conscience*, pp. 192-193.

[21] Jordan, *op. cit.*, Vol. II, p. 260.

groups who remained aloof were the conservative of the Anglicans and those who were more rigid among the Presbyterians. Jordan reports that in 1657 Baxter was seeking to include Baptists in his ecumenical scheme.[22] His movement disappeared, however, after Cromwell's death and the restoration of Charles II. Baxter complained that his latitudinarian conception was "crucified [between the] prophane and formal persecutors on the one hand, and the fanatick dividing sectary [sic]" on the other.[23]

During the reign of Charles II (1660-1685), the ecclesiastical authorities sought to extinguish nonconformity. Independents and Baptists went underground; Presbyterians were driven into the ranks of the nonconformists by the Act of Uniformity of 1662; only the Quakers defied the law openly, at the cost of imprisonment for more than four thousand of their number in 1662 alone.[24] Out of these experiences, principles of an organized nonconformity gradually were developed which later characterized the Free Church movement.

From 1870 the Free Church doctrine underwent a change from an exclusively biblical basis of church order to a position that no system of church discipline and government can be drawn literally from the Scriptures. At the same time, a modification in the interpretation of the sacraments led to a minimizing of their importance, with some concession to participation of laymen in the administering of them. It is conceded by some observers that the theological foundations of the Free Churches were weakened in this period by immanentism and

---

[22] Jordan, *op. cit.,* Vol. III, pp. 336, 339, 342-344; based on Baxter, *Reliquiae Baxterianae,* I, pp. 126, 130-132; *op. cit.,* II, p. 198; _____, *The True Catholic, Works,* XVI, 228; _____, *Confirmation and Restauration, Works,* XIV, 554.

[23] Jordan, *op. cit.,* Vol. III, p. 343.

[24] Herbert S. Skeats and Charles S. Miall, *History of the Free Churches of England, 1688-1891* (London: Alexander & Shepheard, 1891), p. 61.

by the trends in biblical and historical criticism. As a consequence, dissenters became political in their search for spiritual
ends which seemed to be attainable only by secular means.
They tended to repudiate dogmatic theology and the historical elements of the gospel. Christ became for them less a
person who had suffered and died and more an expression
of the divine which is immanently active in all life. Changing
social and religious conditions at the opening of the twentieth
century were forcing Free Churches to change the methods
of their work and to seek some unity. The older idea of the
ministry as Christ's gift to the church was being replaced by
the idea that it is a function of the church and derives its
powers from the congregation. The sermon was no longer
"unquestioned truth," but an expression of the views of the
minister in whom the Spirit of God is immanent.[25]

By the early years of the twentieth century, Congregationalists and Baptists in England "were delegating power to
centralized authorities on a scale unknown in the past."[26]
Illustrative of this trend were the Congregational Union, the
Baptist Union of Great Britain and Ireland, and the interdenominational federation known as the National Council
of Evangelical Free Churches. A parallel trend was in vogue
in the United States where Baptists in the North organized
the Northern Baptist Convention and entered into the Federal
Council of Churches of Christ in America.

About the same time, a renewed interest in the doctrine
of the church was expressed by a number of free churchmen.
In 1911 John Oman's *The Church and the Divine Order* appeared, followed in 1914 by W. B. Selbie's *Nonconformity.*
J. H. Shakespeare wrote *The Churches at the Crossroads*
in 1918. Two years later, A. E. Garvie's *The Holy Catholic*

[25] Grant, *op. cit.,* pp. 71, 77-79; 85, 88, 137-140, 157, 160.
[26] *Ibid.,* p. 184.

Church was published. This series of books led to a renewed interest in the doctrine of the ministry and to a revival of churchmanship. It led also to a restudy of the Free Church viewpoint regarding the relation of the church to the state.

Indeed, a number of restatements of the Free Church position were being formulated. Among these were the writings of P. T. Forsyth, the Congregationalist theologian. He took the position that evangelical dogma needed to be reemphasized by free churchmen since it "is what the Church must believe in order to be a Church."[27] From a strong theological stance, he sought to reconcile freedom and authority within the Free Church tradition. Two other able writers, Edward Shilitto and H. W. Clark, offered a spiritualized interpretation of the nonconformist ideal. Shilitto asserted that "the real principle of Nonconformity . . . is that the life must determine the form."[28] Clark, in a similar vein, defined the nonconformist spirit as that "which exalts life above organization."[29] J. H. Shakespeare, secretary of the Baptist Union and a strong advocate of the union of all Free Churches, became so disturbed by their persistent individualism and declining influence in the years following the First World War that he took the position that denominationalism was outmoded. He was so intent upon a united church to which the modern world might listen that he actually proposed union with the Church of England and reordination.[30]

Among Baptists who were disturbed by Shakespeare's advocacy of reunion was John Clifford, veteran advocate of the

[27] *Ibid.*, p. 232.

[28] E. Shilitto, *The Hope and Mission of the Free Churches* (London: T. C. & E. C. Jack, 1913), p. 16.

[29] H. W. Clark, *History of English Nonconformity* (London: Chapman and Hall, Limited, 1911), Vol. I, p. 3.

[30] J. H. Shakespeare, *The Churches at the Crossroads* (London: Williams and Norgate Press, 1918), pp. 82, 102, 165, 178.

union of Free Churches. Fearful that diversity would be
stifled if Baptists were to join with Episcopalians, Clifford
warned that uniformity was an intolerable burden and un-
necessary to achieve the essential unity of all Christians in
Christ.[31] Although Shakespeare's position was rejected, it
revealed an ambivalence among free churchmen who shared
a common concern for Christian unity but could not agree on
the nature of the unity which they sought.

In the years that followed, independency became identified
with a negative churchmanship which stressed freedom from
sacerdotalism, from external authority, and from tradition.
Free Church leaders began to accommodate themselves to a
scientific approach to the Bible and the world which led them
to a modified view of the church. They came to regard the
purpose of the church as building the kingdom of God. Church
officers became for them organizers of the kingdom. Preaching
became topical and removed from the traditional exposition
of the Scriptures. The sacraments were depreciated, and
church discipline ceased.[32]

Between 1934 and 1940 a Genevan revival, which centered
in Congregationalism in England and in Presbyterianism in
the United States, reasserted the Calvinistic base upon which
nonconformity had always rested. The view was reinstated
that there can be no church without the gospel and no gospel
without the church. The sermon must be a *kerygma* or proclamation of the gospel. The sacraments are seals attached to a
promise which speaks to our condition. In a very real sense,
the Genevan revival "tipped the balance from the freedom
of the Spirit to the objectivity of the Word."[33]

As a consequence, the Free Church position once again

[31] A. C. Underwood, *A History of the English Baptists* (London:
The Carey Kingsgate Press, Ltd., 1947), p. 253.

[32] Grant, *op. cit.*, p. 308.

[33] *Ibid.*, pp. 335, 384.

became theologically oriented. For example, Ernest A. Payne, general secretary of the Baptist Union of Great Britain and Ireland, claimed that the Union was more than a voluntary association of churches; it was an expression of the body of Christ.[34] Leaders within the American Baptist Convention in the United States shared his viewpoint, although their position did not gain wide acceptance among the rank and file of ministers and laymen, for the nineteenth century amalgam of individualism and local autonomy was deeply rooted in Baptist minds. Nonetheless, the deepening of the ecumenical climate at mid-century and thereafter brought Christians of the Free Church tradition into conversation with the more institutional churches. The result has been a furtive effort to reexamine the principles which were forged in a different age in order to determine their current importance and the extent to which they should be retained and shared with the whole church. Even more important has been the question whether the Free Church idea stands in the way of more visible unity among all Christians.

The basic principles inherited by the so-called Free Churches from English nonconformity are sufficiently important to list here for study and reevaluation. They include: (1) The church is not territorially determined in its membership but a fellowship of believers gathered by the Holy Spirit. (2) The church must remain free from control of the state in order to be obedient to her Lord. (3) The reality of the individual's experience with God is basic to vital religion. (4) Organization of the church must always be subordinated to the life of the Spirit. (5) The visible church should seek to maintain a purity of life and faith through a mutual discipline of the members.

[34] Ernest A. Payne, *The Fellowship of Believers* (London: The Carey Kingsgate Press, Ltd., 1952), p. 118.

These essentials of the Free Church witness are no doubt shared to a larger degree than ever before by other communions. It behooves free churchmen, therefore, to determine which of them are still an obstacle to the achievement of more visible unity in the body of Christ. If the ecumenical movement of our day continues to maintain an openness of sharing the respective traditions within the whole church, there may be hope for an inclusion of the best of the Free Church witness into the total faith and life of the people of God.

Chapter 4

FREE CHURCHES
AND CHRISTIAN UNITY

IN THIS DAY of ecumenical dialogue, the questions which need
to be asked include: How have the Free Churches conceived
of Christian unity? To what extent has the ecumenical ideal
been important to them? What, if anything, is there in the
contemporary situation which can enable the Free Churches
to engage more fully and with fewer reservations in conversation with other Christian communions?

We may approach these questions obliquely instead of di-
rectly by listening to what free churchmen have said regarding
the ecumenical ideal. Although there have been evidences of
a Free Church spirit in earlier centuries of the church, we will
find the most fruitful results by beginning with the fifteenth
century. This was a period of cultural renaissance, a time of
a widening appreciation of man's full development of his
capacities in this life, and an era of growing awareness of the
worth of the individual and hence of the humanist tradition.
It was an epoch in the history of Christianity when the old
order of institutionalism and medieval conformity were being

challenged by new voices, some deeply Christian, others virtually secular. A spirit of liberation was in the air; yet with it there was still prevailing a profound respect for the unity of Christendom.

Among the literary men of the fifteenth century were those, humanistic in point of view, who saw this unity of Christendom through medieval eyes. For example, Nicholas Cusa (1401-1464) wrote in 1433 his book, *De concordentia catholica*, in which he pleaded for love of the Church, the Empire, and the Sacrament. He worked at the Council of Florence (1439) for the union of the Greek Orthodox Church with Rome. He also labored for the reconciliation of the Hussites with the Roman See between 1450 and 1452. Because he felt that it was impossible for anyone to gain a full knowledge of absolute truth, he held that one must be tolerant of alternate viewpoints. He even described Judaism, Christianity, and Mohammedanism as different aspects of the same road to God.

In his last book, *Cribatio Alchornani,* Cusa examined the usefulness of the Koran for a Christian understanding of the gospel. He concluded that the revelation, presented first by Moses, and more fully and perfectly by Christ, had been poorly followed by Mohammed. When Constantinople fell to the Turks in 1453, he urged a discussion between Christians and Moslems. He even envisioned the possibility of achieving ultimate unity among peoples of diverse views. Unity, he said, should be sought on the basis of great common truths, not on the basis of divergent rites and ceremonies.[1]

A similar trend of thought appears in the writing of Marsilius Ficinus (1433-1499), head of the Florentine Academy and a disciple of Platonism. In his principal works, *Theologia Platonica* and *De Christiana Religione,* he sought to show that

[1] Joseph Lecler, S. J., *Histoire de la Tolérance au Siècle de la Réforme* (Paris: Aubier, 1955), Vol. I, pp. 127-130.

the Platonist philosophers were approaching Christ. Indeed, like Cusa, he found in non-Christian philosophers and religions much in common with Christianity. In chapter four of *De Christiana Religione,* he concluded that every sincere religion, however imperfect, is pleasing to God, although he conceded that there is more truth in some religions than in others.[2]

Ficinus' pupil, Pico della Mirandola (1463-1494), is known for his *Conclusions Philosophiques,* some nine hundred theses which he raised and answered, thirteen of which were condemned by Pope Innocent III. Pico was consumed with the idea of one great doctrinal synthesis which reconciled under the aegis of the Christian faith the systems of philosophy and religion that differ from and even appear to oppose Christianity. His premature death interrupted his task of constructing a new synthesis which would have embraced even the Mystery Cults of the East and ancient magic as well as Greek and Hebrew thought, for in them he thought he had found various approaches to the religion of Christ. From this base, he would have moved to create a universal religion to unite all men.[3]

We mention these representative voices, not because they are typical of the Free Church approach to Christianity, which is evangelical, but because their broad Christian tolerance is a part of the Free Church spirit to this day. Indeed, there is tension within the Free Church movement between the broadly tolerant wing and those who turn with misgivings away from the religious indifferentism which they think they see in the ecumenical movement.

In the sixteenth century, further encouragement was given to the ecumenical ideal by the Protestant reformers. Among

2 *Ibid.,* pp. 130-131.
3 *Ibid.,* pp. 131-132.

these was Desiderius Erasmus (1466 or 1469-1536) who combined within his thought the best of the humanist tradition with a deep devotion to the Roman Catholic Church of his fathers. As a humanist, he was committed to finding unity within the Church. To be a party to schism was therefore, in his eyes, a scandal and a folly. His error was to have underestimated the place of doctrine in Luther's opposition to the Catholic Church. Being more humanist than theologian, Erasmus believed that it was possible to recover a common basis of faith in the simplicity of the primitive Church. The development of dogma in the Medieval Church he regarded as an evil necessity. He proposed civil toleration of Protestantism, not because he saw religious liberty as an ideal, but because he believed that toleration was a form of patience and Christian love by which to return to unity.[4]

Still another Christian humanist to encourage the search for Christian unity was Georges Cassander (1513-1566), an admirer of Erasmus and author of a work against dissidence in religion, *De Officio Pii ac Publicae Tranquillitatis Vere Amantis Viri in Hoc Religionis Dissidio.* Like the irenic Erasmians, he aspired to a restoration of a united Christianity under the protection of the princes, but he did not advocate civil toleration by indifference to confessional faith. He rejected the severity of the Evangelicals in suppressing variations of belief. He condemned both theologians who resorted to heresy-hunting to protect the unity of the Church and those who separated from the Church in order to bear their witness to the faith. He believed that unity should be achieved by placing emphasis upon fundamentals of the faith, and not by making differences among the churches an obstacle to union in love.[5]

[4] *Ibid.*, pp. 146-149.
[5] *Ibid.*, pp. 268-270.

Perhaps the most illustrious ecumenical voice of the sixteenth century was Hugo Grotius (1583-1645), a Dutch jurist and a Protestant churchman of wide connections in European countries. In his last years he developed his great design for Christian unity in a book entitled *Via ad Pacem Ecclesiasticam* (1642). Like Cassander, he sought to unite the churches on the basis of fundamental articles. He saw in the intolerance of Calvinism a major factor contributing to divisions. Although an Arminian, he believed that the Roman Catholic Church possessed the true fundamentals necessary to salvation; but by its moral laxness, the abuse of Aristotelian Scholasticism, and the papal abuse of power, it fell short of providing the way to unity.[6]

However, it was in England where the Free Church movement found congenial soil and grew against great odds. Within the Church of England were men who sought to renew its spiritual life while preserving its unity. Such a man was Bishop Thomas Cranmer, who believed firmly that doctrinal uniformity was essential to true unity. Yet, he was ready to waive minor differences to achieve this goal. Professor Jordan of Harvard has observed that the realization of Cranmer's ideal was impossible, at least until Christians were willing "to insist upon the spiritual nature of Christianity as opposed to the unyielding shell of doctrinal accretion."[7]

The Anabaptists supplied the religious argument against persecution. They insisted that persecution was foreign to the nature and meaning of Christianity. They distinguished between civil and spiritual offenses. They regarded differences of opinion in matters of religion as legitimate. For them the word of God was a sufficient guide; when it did not clearly speak, each man could choose for himself.

English Baptists, influenced in part by the Anabaptist doc-

6 *Ibid.*, Vol. II, pp. 276-279.
7 Jordan, *op. cit.*, Vol. I, p. 72.

trine and in part by Calvinistic teaching, regarded the church universal as becoming visible in the congregations of true believers, but they refused to confine the identity of this church universal to any single ecclesiastical organization. Like Calvin, they did not think of the church as having attained perfection, but as moving toward perfection. Therefore perfection in holiness was not for them a mark of the church. In the Second London Confession of 1677, the Calvinistic or Particular Baptists witnessed to the presence in the world of a visible church, however imperfect:

> The purest Churches under heaven are subject to mixture, and error; and som [sic] have so degenerated as to become no Churches of Christ, but Synagogues of Satan; nevertheless Christ always hath had, and ever shall have a Kingdome, in this world, to the end thereof, of such as believe in him, and make profession of his name.[8]

The General Baptists expressed a similar point of view in their "Orthodox Creed" of 1678:

> Altho' there may be many errors in such a visible church, or congregations, they being not infallible, yet those errors being not fundamental, and the church in the major, or governing part, being not guilty, she is not thereby unchurched; nevertheless she ought to detect those errors, and to reform, according to God's holy word, and from such visible church, or congregations, no man ought by any pretence whatever, schismatically to separate.[9]

The same creed affirmed that general councils or assemblies, composed of representatives of the member congregations, "make but one church, and have lawful right, and suffrage in this general meeting, or assembly, to act in the name of Christ . . . to preserve unity, to prevent heresy, and superintendency among, or in any congregation whatsoever within its own limits, or jurisdiction."[10] Thus did the English Baptist

[8] W. J. McGlothlin, *Baptist Confessions of Faith* (Valley Forge: The Judson Press, 1911), pp. 264-265.

[9] *Ibid.*, p. 146.

[10] *Ibid.*, p. 154.

movement seek to recover the New Testament balance between the universal and the local aspects of the church, preserving the sense of the oneness of the people of God in the congregation while not losing sight of the wholeness of the church.

One of the most ecumenically minded Baptists of the seventeenth century was John Bunyan (1628-1688). Converted at the age of twenty-five at Bedford, he was baptized by John Gifford, the local Baptist minister. Three years later he was ordained on the insistence of his fellow Baptists and called to be their pastor. Because he preached what he felt, and that with eloquence and literary imagination, he became very popular, a fact which helps to explain the long imprisonment which he suffered from 1660 to 1672 for preaching without a license. Upon gaining his freedom, he resumed his pastorate in Bedford.

Bunyan adopted an open membership policy, refusing to require mature Christians of other communions to receive believer's baptism in order to unite with his congregation. When his liberal position was denounced by London Baptists, he defended it in a book published in 1673 under the title, *Differences in Judgment about Water Baptism No Bar to Communion.* In it he wrote:

> All I say is that the Church of Christ hath not warrant to keep out of their communion the Christian that is discovered to be a visible saint by the Word, the Christian that walketh according to his light with God. . . . Christ, not Baptism, is the way to the sheepfold. . . .[11]

In 1684 he wrote further on behalf of Christian unity in another book entitled, *A Holy Life in the Beauty of Christianity:*

[11] Marcus L. Loane, *Makers of Religious Freedom in the Seventeenth Century* (Grand Rapids: Wm. B. Eerdmans Publishing Co., 1961), pp. 139-140; cited from George Offor, *The Works of John Bunyan,* Vol. II, pp. 617, 634. Used by permission.

> It is strange to see at this day how, notwithstanding all the threatenings of God, men are wedded to their own opinions beyond what the law of grace and love will admit. Here is a Presbyter, here is an Independent, and a Baptist, so joined each man to his own opinion that they can not have that communion one with another as by the testament of the Lord Jesus they are commanded and enjoined. What is the cause? Is the truth? No! God is the author of no confusion in the Church of God. It is because every man makes too much of his own opinion.[12]

Political necessity as well as theological conviction contributed to the development of a degree of unity among the Free Churches. The renewal of persecution after 1660, when the Church of England sought to suppress dissent by the Clarendon Code, brought Baptists and Congregationalists nearer to Presbyterians. Dissenters found it necessary to present a united front. One way was to show doctrinal agreement. The famed Westminster Confession, adopted by the Presbyterian General Assembly in 1648, was proof of this. In fact, the Particular Baptists of London and vicinity sought to demonstrate their agreement with Presbyterians and Congregationalists by making the Westminster Confession the basis of a new confession of their own in 1677. The Baptist confession was in reality a modification of the Presbyterian creed produced by William Collins, pastor of the Petty France Church in London, and adopted by representatives of the churches in England and Wales. The Lord's Supper was not restricted to persons who have been baptized as believers as it was in the 1644 London Baptist Confession. Several editions of this 1677 document were issued in the years that followed. A condensation prepared by Benjamin Keach in 1697 became the substance of the Philadelphia Confession of 1742.

The Second London Confession of Particular Baptists (1677) admitted in its section on the church that while the

---

[12] *Ibid.*, pp. 140-141; cited from *Works*, Vol. II, p. 538.

universal church is invisible, all persons professing faith in the gospel and obedience to Christ are visible saints and are to be found in congregations which, however pure, are subject to mixture and error. The conclusion is that this visible church has authenticity in spite of its imperfection. The General Baptists expressed the same thought in stronger words in their "Orthodox Creed" (1678) by describing the universal church as "the visible church of Christ on earth, . . . made up of several distinct congregations, which make up that one catholick [sic] church, or mystical body of Christ."[13]

A careful reading of early records reveals that Baptists of the seventeenth century placed a premium on the ideal of Christian unity, but sought it within the framework of their understanding of the primitive faith and practice of the New Testament. When, for example, Philadelphia Baptists received on September 26, 1698, from Thomas Clayton, an Anglican clergyman recently arrived in the city, an invitation to return to the Church of England, they affirmed their endorsement of Christian unity as an ideal but insisted on the preservation of their emphasis upon a strict biblicism. In a document prepared under the date of March 11, 1699, they explained:

> That to rend from a rightly constituted church of Christ is that which our souls abhor; and that love, peace and unity with all christians and concord and agreement in the true faith and worship of God are that which we greatly desire. . . . nor are we at all averse to a reconciliation with the church of England, provided it can be proved by the holy scriptures that her constitution, orders, officers, worship and service are of divine appointment, and not of human invention.[14]

[13] William L. Lumpkin, *Baptist Confessions of Faith* (Valley Forge: The Judson Press, 1959), pp. 318-319.

[14] Morgan Edwards, *Materials Towards a History of the Baptists in Pennsylvania*, Vol. I (Philadelphia, 1770), pp. 99-103, cited in H. Shelton Smith, *et al.*, *American Christianity: An Historical Interpretation with Representative Documents* (New York: Charles Scribner's Sons, 1960), Vol. I, p. 269.

Some, however, were unwilling to let their emphases stand in the way of the wider Christian fellowship. Among these was John Bunyan, to whom we have referred already, and Thomas Hollis, a hardware merchant of London and a deacon in an open membership church which met in Pinner's Hall. Although he was identified with the Particular Baptists and the first treasurer of the Particular Baptist Fund for ministerial education, he was in no sense a strict Calvinist. It is said that when the Reverend Jeremiah Hunt became his pastor in 1707, they maintained a close friendship in spite of the fact that Hunt was not a Calvinist and disclaimed openly the doctrine of the Trinity. Further indication of his liberal views may be seen from the fact that when he established two professorial chairs at Harvard College, he insisted that no sectarian requirements be placed on the incumbents.[15]

One of the ablest exponents of the ecumenical ideal in this period was Richard Baxter (1615-1691), Puritan preacher, politician and negotiator. Very early in his ministry within the Church of England, he became troubled by the persecuting spirit of ecclesiastical conformists on the one hand and by the censorious, often divisive, spirit of nonconformists on the other. During the Civil War (1642-1649) he served as a chaplain in Cromwell's army. When illness overtook him in 1646, he returned to his pastorate at Kidderminster and undertook through writing and negotiations to secure peace and harmony among the Puritans.

On May 7, 1652, Baxter wrote to John Dury (1596-1680), an ardent ecumenist, proposing a conference of representatives from the Anglican, Presbyterian, and Independent parties. It was his belief that a church union could be developed to accommodate even Arminians and Baptists. Such an unofficial conference took place on April 2, 1654, in London with only

[15] David A. MacQueen, "Thomas Hollis—Early Baptist Benefactor," in *The Chronicle,* Vol. 6, No. 2 (April, 1943), pp. 80-82.

five Presbyterians and five Independents in attendance. Returning home, Baxter worked for a church union on the local level through a voluntary association which had been projected in Worcestershire in 1652. He joined with John Gauden, an Anglican clergyman, in advocating a reduction of the bishops' powers in a new national church which they hoped might include Anglicans and Puritan nonconformists. When Charles II was restored to his throne in 1660, Baxter and the Presbyterians hoped for a national church which would be comprehensive of limited episcopacy and many of the features of the Presbyterian Kirk of Scotland. Failure of the Savoy Conference earlier in 1662, and passage of the Act of Uniformity on May 19, 1662, doomed such a plan to restore church unity by its insistence on episcopal ordination, consent of the Book of Common Prayer, and renunciation of the Solemn League.[16]

When the Stuarts were finally ousted in 1689 in favor of a constitutional monarchy with William and Mary of Orange, the liberal spirit extended to religion. By an Act of Toleration, Parliament guaranteed a measure of religious freedom for nonconformists. This partial victory had the effect of lessening the intensity of their vigor. Yet, the very spirit of toleration encouraged a liberal attitude toward denominational differences which paved the way for eventual achievements in re-uniting a badly divided Protestantism. At the same time the necessity of winning further relief from liabilities placed upon the nonconformist churches encouraged cooperation and the attainment of a united front. This spirit was evident, for example, among the Baptists of Berkshire who, it is reported:

> believed in the Church, holy, catholic and apostolic, but were certain that it must find local, visible embodiment in companies of believing men and women, drawing strength from Word and sacrament, assist-

[16] James C. Spalding and Maynard F. Brass, "Reduction of Episcopacy as a Means to Unity in England, 1640-1662," in *Church History*, Vol. 30, No. 4 (December, 1961), pp. 414-432.

ing one another in the attempt to live the Christian life, but free from the control of civil authorities.[17]

Further illustration may be seen in the Northern Association of Particular Baptists, which in 1798 participated with ministers of different denominations at Hamsterly, in the county of Durham, in adopting these resolutions:

> To unite with all evangelical ministers, who believe and preach the leading and fundamental doctrines of the Gospel; and not to suffer any difference of opinion, in other matters of less importance, to form a barrier to so desirable a union.[18]

In 1817 at the instigation of Dr. F. A. Cox, pastor of the Baptist church in Hackney, a meeting of representatives of all Protestant denominations was held in London under the presidency of the Duke of Sussex "to celebrate the third century of the Protestant Reformation."[19]

The new liberality was not confined to free churchmen. It was expressed also by Frederick W. Robertson (1816-1853), the broad-gauged Anglican pulpiteer of Brighton. For him the living Christ was central, not a mere image of his authority or a notion about him. He regarded creeds as "aids to faith" but not to be tolerated as limitations placed upon faith. He looked forward "to an advance of the Christian Church—not into new truths, but into wider and more tolerant views of those old truths which in themselves are incapable of change."[20]

[17] Ernest A. Payne, *The Baptists of Berkshire Through Three Centuries* (London: The Carey Kingsgate Press, Ltd., 1951), p. 140.

[18] *The Baptist Register, 1798-1801,* Vol. IV (English publication), p. 86.

[19] John Stoughton, *History of Religion in England* (London: Hodder and Stoughton, Limited, 1901), Vol. VII, pp. 281-282.

[20] John Tulloch, *Movements of Religious Thought in Britain During the Nineteenth Century* (New York: Charles Scribner's Sons, 1885), p. 318.

During the nineteenth century the Free Churches experienced their greatest progress in growth within their home territory, whether in Britain or in the United States. The political and cultural climate facilitated a favorable response to their stress upon the individual and the freedom of the church from interference with its divinely appointed mission. At the same time, their evangelical emphasis encouraged their numerical growth at home and their success abroad in founding new churches through overseas missionary ventures. The Methodists, Baptists, Presbyterians, Congregationalists, and Disciples of Christ were increasing in prominence and size, especially in the United States. The fact that the cause of religious liberty had been won in America meant that there was little distinction in this emphasis between the traditional Free Churches and the other major Protestant bodies like the Lutherans and the Episcopalians. The differences with respect to these latter communions involved other matters such as creedal uniformity and the episcopate.

In the survey of the Free Church tradition, the development of cooperative efforts among the Free Churches in Britain during the nineteenth century was noted. There was a parallel trend in the United States in the same period. During the first quarter of the century, the evangelical Protestant denominations, counterpart of the Free Churches in England, manifested a marked spirit of unity. Indeed, interdenominational cooperation was evident in numerous societies such as the American Bible Society, the General Tract Society, and the American Home Mission Society. Then in the 1820's and the 1830's the "evangelical united front," as this combination of denominations has been called, began to weaken before a resurgence of sectarianism, a resistance on the frontier to the leadership of the voluntary societies whose headquarters were in the East, the rise of anti-mission opposition to human efforts to win people to Christ, and the slavery issue.

The resurgence of sectarianism occurred in a number of denominations, apparently in response to a desire to recover authentic ecclesiastical authority in place of the broadly tolerant interdenominational expression of Christianity which had been developing through voluntary societies in which laymen played a prominent role. Among Episcopalians it was a High Church party that sought to recover the liturgical and sacramental character of the medieval tradition. Among Presbyterians, it was an Old School party which opposed the revivalism of the New School Presbyterians who seemed more interested in a pietistic religious experience than in a sound theological understanding of the Christian faith. Among Lutherans it was a confessional movement which sought to restore an emphasis upon the theological foundations of the church. Among Baptists it was an emphasis on the part of some to restore the "old landmarks" of New Testament Christianity as a way of establishing their identity as the true successors of the primitive church. The exponents of Landmarkism contended that only Baptist congregations constituted true Christianity, because they manifested the marks of a gospel church in Jerusalem. There was no doubt in the minds of Landmark Baptists that this early Christian church was a Baptist church, purely local in character and composed only of persons baptized as believers by immersion.[21]

This response among Protestants to an authentic rootage in their respective ecclesiastical traditions may be seen in varying degrees as something of a corrective to the effects of revivalism which shaped American Protestantism in the eighteenth and early nineteenth centuries. The great revivals

[21] Lefferts A. Loetscher, "The Problem of Christian Unity in Early Nineteenth-Century America," in *Church History*, Vol. 32, No. 1 (March, 1963), pp. 13-14. For a description of Landmarkism see the author's account in Winthrop S. Hudson, ed., *Baptist Concepts of the Church* (Valley Forge: The Judson Press, 1959), pp. 170-195.

of this period, with their marked emotional appeal for personal conversion and their stress upon the religious response of the individual, had weakened a sense of need for the church and had distorted the biblical importance of the community of faith as the body of Christ. It was all too easy for the revivalist to think that the church was a convenience for those who were saved, but in no sense indispensable to the development of the Christian life. Thus, the effort of some denominations to recover a loyalty to the church and their respective traditions was intended to be a corrective. But, like so many correctives, the emphasis swung to an extreme which only served to deepen for a time the divisions in Protestantism.

The trend had been deepened also by the very success of the Free Churches' efforts to achieve within the nation a freedom from coercion in matters of religion. The strong element of dissent within American Protestantism had found an ally in the spirit of the enlightenment as expressed by Thomas Jefferson, James Madison, and others of the founding fathers who believed in the complete separation of the church and the state in the national government. Out of the combination of these forces with American culture came what one historian has called the American "emphasis upon the churches rather than upon the Church. In a country that lacked a unity of cultural tradition and any single religious basis for the Federal Constitution, it was only natural that religious life should be marked by a variety of autonomous churches and denominations."[22]

Following the Civil War (1861-1865), however, the practical need for interdenominational cooperation came again to the fore. A flood of immigrants was increasing the religious pluralism of American society. Protestants were hard pressed, especially in the Northeast and Midwest, to serve these

[22] Cyril C. Richardson, *The Church Through the Centuries* (New York: Charles Scribner's Sons, 1938), p. 225.

Europeans whose ties with Christianity were tenuous, if not entirely broken, and at the same time to win back to the church a generation of Americans who had moved from the farms into the burgeoning industrial centers to find employment and excitement. City mission societies were established; city-wide evangelistic crusades were launched on an interdenominational basis; and efforts at moral and social reform were made jointly by Protestant leaders.

The revivalism which had weakened the recovery of Christian unity through the church by its encouragement of a religion of personal experience that minimized the necessity of the church and of theology had also become the source of energy for the great missionary crusade of the nineteenth century. And out of that missionary effort, wrought through the voluntary societies of many denominations, came the primary stimulus to the modern ecumenical movement.

Kenneth Scott Latourette, noted American church historian, observes that missionaries working in India and China began assembling in interdenominational conferences for the effective prosecution of their tasks in the second half of the nineteenth century.[23] After World War I this development took the form of national Christian councils organized in many lands and regions, including India, China, Japan, and the Near East. Meanwhile at home, the sending churches organized in 1893 the Foreign Missions Conference of North America. In 1908 the Home Missions Council was formed to plan ecumenically for the United States. In 1912 the Conference of Missionary Societies of Great Britain and Ireland was constituted.

Such interdenominational cooperation eventuated in a World Missionary Conference held at Edinburgh in 1910. It

[23] For an excellent brief survey of the modern ecumenical movement, see Kenneth Scott Latourette, *The Emergence of a World Christian Community* (New Haven: Yale University Press, 1949), pp. 22-56.

proved to be the fulfillment of a long-cherished dream of William Carey, the British Baptist pioneer of Protestant foreign missions. He had proposed in 1810 that a series of such conferences be held every ten years. The spirit of the Edinburgh Conference was kept alive by John R. Mott, a Christian layman who, as chairman of a Continuation Committee, led in planning a series of such conferences in several lands on the eve of World War I. In 1921 the International Missionary Council was organized to coordinate the work of twenty-six missionary organizations from all five continents and Australasia. In time, it grew in membership and functioned somewhat as a central planning board for Protestant missions.

The concern for the Christian instruction and care of children and youth also drew Protestants together in a number of organizations. Among these were the various Sunday school unions and societies of the nineteenth century which culminated in the World's Sunday School Association formed in 1907 (since 1947 called the World Council of Christian Education). The Young Men's Christian Associations, first conceived in London in 1844, spread to the United States and eventually around the world. In 1895 the World's Student Christian Federation and the World's Christian Endeavor Union drew young people from many denominations.

The concept of federations or councils of churches was developed chiefly in the twentieth century. The organization of the Federal Council of Churches of Christ in America was constituted in 1908. By 1948 its membership included religious bodies which together had slightly more than half of the Protestant church membership in the nation. In 1950 the Federal Council was merged with several other interdenominational agencies into the National Council of Churches. The British Council of Churches (1942), which includes in its membership the Church of England, the Church of Scotland,

and most of the Free Churches, has already been mentioned. The most comprehensive of these councils of churches is the World Council of Churches, which was constituted provisionally in 1938 at Utrecht, in the Netherlands, and formally organized at Amsterdam in 1948. It grew from 125 church bodies to 232 churches in 1968. It includes not only Protestant communions, but Old Catholic churches, several of the Eastern Orthodox Churches, the Coptic Church, the Syrian (Jacobite) Church, the Nestorians, and part of the Syrian Church of India.

Still another phase of the movement for Christian unity has been church union. The most common examples have been the merger of different branches of the same denominational family, as the formation of the United Lutheran Church in 1917 and 1918, the Methodist Church in England in 1932, and the Methodist Church in the United States in 1939. Then there have been mergers of denominations of different traditions, as the United Church of Canada formed in 1925 by the union of Methodists, Presbyterians, and Congregationalists; or as the Church of Christ in China, constituted in the same year around a Presbyterian nucleus which eventually included Baptists, Congregationalists, Methodists, and United Brethren. Other examples include the Church of Christ in Japan (1941) and the Church of South India (1947), which embraced former Anglicans, Congregationalists, Methodists, Presbyterians, and Reformed. The most notable effort along this line at the present time is the Consultation on Church Union, which began in 1962 with four denominations and which included in 1968 nine communions in an effort to form "a united church, truly catholic, truly evangelical, and truly reformed." The participants include the United Presbyterian Church in the U. S. A., the Presbyterian Church in the U. S., the Protestant Episcopal Church, the United Church of Christ, the Methodist Church, the Disciples of Christ, the Evangelical

United Brethren Church, the African Methodist Episcopal Church, the African Methodist Episcopal Zion Church, and the Christian Methodist Episcopal Church.[24]

It should be noted that the movement toward Christian unity arose out of a dual purpose characteristic of the churches in the nineteenth century; namely, a strong missionary impulse and a practical belief that this could be done better through interdenominational cooperation. Since the Free Churches were in the vanguard in the missionary movement, it is not surprising that they made a significant contribution to cooperative Protestant endeavors. The rationale to justify their participation in the ecumenical movement stopped short, in many cases, of a readiness to go beyond federations and councils of churches to full ecclesiastical union. There has remained within the Free Churches to the present time a tendency to spiritualize Christian unity and a reticence to objectify it in visible union lest the organizational structure obscure the spiritual reality and inhibit the freedom of the people of God to be led by the Holy Spirit.

Yet, there are indications that the churches of a congregational polity are undergoing change. They are finding that the inefficiencies of a decentralized church life are too costly in a highly-structured technological society. These churches, which constituted roughly half of American Protestantism at mid-century, include Baptists, Congregationalists, Disciples of Christ, and numerous smaller groups. All of them are committed to forms of church polity centering in the local congregation. Many of them are reluctant to reevaluate their rationale for congregationalism because it is for them rooted in the very nature of New Testament Christianity and because it has had such an enormously successful appeal in the frontier era of American life. Yet each of these church bodies has

[24] See *Consultation on Church Union 1967* (Cincinnati: Forward Movement Publications, 1967).

become increasingly uneasy about its inability to function effectively in the new age. Their denominational leaders find local autonomy and decentralized administration cumbersome, wasteful, and a hindrance to effective Christian mission. At the same time, new biblical insights show that the New Testament provides no single pattern of church polity.

Within each of the denominations mentioned are those who urge a shift of center "from a fragmented, loosely related association of independent congregations sharing a common name and assorted tenets and practices toward a more tightly structured and representatively administered body—from local autonomy toward unified government, from churches to church."[25] One of these church bodies, the International Convention of Christian Churches (Disciples of Christ) took decisive action at its Dallas assembly in September, 1966, which reflects this trend. The Convention voted to convert the denomination's mass assembly to a delegated body. It received a "Provisional Design for the Christian Church" which was widely discussed across the nation and presented in revised form to the 1967 Assembly which recommended it for approval, with adoption expected in 1968. Its effect will be to unify the denomination's autonomous agencies and congregations in a single "Church." These steps toward representative government and centralized administration are intended to heighten the Disciples' sense of oneness in mission and will have the effect of preparing them to participate more responsibly in the Consultation on Church Union.[26]

[25] Editorial, *The Christian Century*, Vol. 83, No. 41 (October 12, 1966), p. 1231.

[26] *Ibid.*, pp. 1231-32. For trends among Baptists, see Paul M. Harrison, *Authority and Power in the Free Church Tradition; A Social Case Study of the American Baptist Convention* (Princeton: Princeton University Press, 1959); and Samuel S. Hill, Jr., and Robert G. Torbet, *Baptists — North and South* (Valley Forge: The Judson Press, 1964).

Thus we see among the Free Churches a move toward correcting the Protestant imbalance on the side of decentralization at a time when the Roman Catholic Church, in accord with decisions made by the Second Vatican Council, is moving slowly from a position of absolute power and monolithic centralization to correct to some extent, at least, the Catholic imbalance on the side of monarchical control. That this dual process is proceeding simultaneously is a factor which may enhance the possibility of better understanding between Christians of widely divergent traditions and so improve the witness of the whole Christian Church in the eyes of the world.

Chapter 5

AN AMBIVALENT APPROACH
TO CHRISTIAN UNITY

BECAUSE THE FREE CHURCHES historically comprised a radical
protest against the authoritarianism, institutional rigidity, and
identification with the state which characterized the Medieval
Catholic Church, their stance with respect to the current
ecumenical movement is marked by ambivalence. On the one
hand, they are conditioned by their history to approach with
caution any move toward union with communions which are
committed to an ecclesiastical hierarchy, to doctrinal and
liturgical uniformity, and to a connection with the state. On
the other hand, they are increasingly aware of the need for
greater unity of witness among Christians in the face of major
dangers to the survival of humanity itself, and many would
like to affirm their Free Church principles within the ecumenical movement rather than from without.

The fact is that Free Churches are divided in their approach
to Christian unity. Some are frankly sectarian and opposed to
any move towards healing of old divisions. Some seek a "safe"
measure of cooperation with other churches in councils or

federations which do not endanger their basic identity and convictions. Others are ready to reevaluate their historic development in order to find a basis for reunion with other churches. It is no understatement to say that the road to the reunion of a fragmented Christianity is especially difficult for those whose principles were the most radical and who therefore have the most to concede in the restoration of unity.

To illustrate this problem for the Free Churches and the manner in which some have moved toward its solution, the approaches of two representative denominations are described in this chapter and the next. The first for examination is the Baptist denomination, one of the very large free church bodies. This group includes free churchmen who are quite sectarian, as well as those who seek to bear their witness as a part of the church universal. The second is the Disciples of Christ, which began to develop in the 1800's as a restorationist movement in American Christianity. Like the Baptists, they sought to restore the purity of the church in keeping with the primitive pattern of the New Testament. But unlike the Baptists, they were committed to being a uniting church. Impatient with creedal barriers to unity, they sought a renewed church on the simple basis of the biblical commitment to Jesus Christ as Lord, to which they bore witness in believer's baptism. For a brief period they joined forces with the Baptists, but eventually withdrew to form their own fellowship. Although they faced some of the same problems as the Baptists in their church life, they were from the beginning committed to the realization of the wholeness of the church, whereas the Baptists were not agreed on this objective.

This chapter will consider the ambivalence which is inherent in the attitude of many Free Churches towards Christian unity, using the Baptists as an illustration. As noted in Chapter Two, the particularity, exclusivism, and independency which marked Puritan Congregationalism also characterized the Baptist churches which emerged from it. For them the norm of the true church was to be found in primitive Christianity, according to which the most telling mark was the covenanting community of committed disciples gathered by the direct work of the Holy Spirit. The external sign of this community was believer's baptism, which became the safeguard to a "pure church" in which each member, without coercion, had responded in faith and obedience to Christ as Lord. Although some early Baptists, like John Bunyan, refused to allow this act to divide them from other Christians, baptism did serve to separate Baptists from other churches. Accordingly, the sectarianism inherent in their view of the church colored the concern for the unity of the church which they affirmed in their confessional statements.

This ambivalence which was typical of many Free Churches was also the product of a fear that diversity would be stifled by union with churches that required doctrinal, liturgical, and ecclesiastical uniformity. This attitude was evident among Baptists, Congregationalists, and others in seventeenth-century England.[1] For them the church universal became visible in the congregations of true believers, but they refused to confine the identity of the church universal to any single ecclesiastical organization. While they valued the ideal of Christian unity, they sought it within the framework of their understanding of the primitive faith and life of the New Testament.

This approach to Christian unity may be understood in part, at least, by reflection upon the initial Baptist response to the ecumenical ideal in England and its later developments within the United States.

THE ECUMENICAL IDEAL AMONG EARLY BAPTISTS

Among early Baptist confessions of faith, there is an absence

[1] See Chapter Three.

of narrowly sectarian definitions of the church in either the Anabaptist confession of the sixteenth century or the English Baptist statements of the seventeenth century. The renewal of persecution of dissenters which followed the restoration of Charles II in 1660 after the respite enjoyed under the Commonwealth brought Baptists, Congregationalists, and Presbyterians nearer to each other. William L. Lumpkin observes in his new edition of *Baptist Confessions of Faith* that, "it was important that Dissenters form a united front, which might be demonstrated by a show of doctrinal agreement among themselves."[2] The document on which they displayed their essential unity was the Westminster Confession (1646), which became the basis of the Second London Confession prepared by the Particular Baptists (Calvinists) of London and vicinity and approved by representatives of sister churches in England and Wales in a general meeting in 1677. This confession distinguished between "the Catholick or universal Church," which is invisible, and the visible churches, the purest of which "are subject to mixture, and error."[3] An appendix to this confession contains a statement which is especially indicative of the ecumenical spirit of these Particular Baptists:

And although we do differ from our brethren who are Paedobaptists; in the subject and administration of Baptisme [sic], and after such other circumstances as have a necessary dependence on our observance of that Ordinance, . . . yet we would not be from hence misconstrued, as if the discharge of our own consciences herein, did any wayes [sic] disoblige or alienate our affections, or conversations from any others that fear the Lord.[4]

Further evidence of the ecumenical ideal in early Baptist tradition may be seen in the fact that Baptists were pioneers,

[2] Lumpkin, *op. cit.*, p. 236.
[3] *Ibid.*, p. 285.
[4] McGlothlin, *op. cit.*, p. 275.

through William Carey and his successors, in creating a world outreach for the Christian gospel. Carey's proposal in 1810 for interdenominational missionary conferences every ten years came to fruition in the International Missionary Council over a century later.

THE DEVELOPMENT OF THE SPIRIT OF ISOLATION

The general spirit of Baptists in early American life was congenial to interdenominational cooperation. As a matter of fact, their minority status in colonies where a state church prevailed stimulated friendly recognition of other communions, particularly the Presbyterians, as allies in a common crusade for religious liberty. From the Philadelphia Baptist Association the English Baptist tradition spread to New England and to the South. Not until the early nineteenth century did the church come to be defined in purely local terms, a fact which laid the foundation for the isolationist attitude of many Baptists toward the ecumenical movement which emerged after 1900.

The leading exponents of the local church view were Francis Wayland, J. Newton Brown, J. R. Graves, and Edward T. Hiscox. Wayland, president of Brown University in Providence, Rhode Island, and an important spokesman for foreign missions, insisted on what he called the "absolute independence of the churches." He argued that the Baptist missionary enterprise should be sustained by benevolent societies of interested individuals, not by churches; for churches could not delegate authority to a higher ecclesiastical body.[5]

In many respects Wayland typified the viewpoint of most Baptists of his time concerning the church. When, for example, the Board of the newly organized New Hampshire Baptist Convention (1826) approved a confessional statement

[5] Francis Wayland, *Notes on the Principles and Practices of Baptist Churches* (New York: Sheldon & Co., 1867), pp. 165, 177, 189, 191.

in 1833, it embodied a definition of the church which was solely in terms of the local congregation of baptized believers. Immersion was made a prerequisite to church membership and to the observance of the Lord's Supper. Known as the New Hampshire Declaration of Faith, it received wide publicity and gained general acceptance when, twenty years later, the Reverend J. Newton Brown, one of its coauthors, revised it and incorporated it in a *Baptist Church Manual.* This he did on his own authority as book editor of The American Baptist Publication Society. For the next half century, this confessional statement became the most commonly accepted expression of Baptist beliefs in the United States. Being only moderately Calvinistic and supporting a local view of the church, it supplanted in influence the more strictly Calvinistic Philadelphia Baptist Confession.[6]

At the midcentury, the local concept of the church was given further support from a new direction. J. R. Graves, a New Englander who rejected the idea of the universal church, advanced a teaching which came to be known as Landmarkism. He was active from 1845 until his death in 1893 in Tennessee, first as school teacher and pastor in Nashville, and then as editor of *The Tennessee Baptist,* which he moved to Memphis after the Civil War and reestablished as *The Baptist.* He advanced a rigidly local view of the church, and sought to establish an historic succession of true Baptist churches from the first congregation of Christians at Jerusalem until the present time. He conceived his mission to be the resetting of the "Old Landmarks," by which he meant *"those principles which all true Baptists, in all ages, have professed to believe."*[7]

[6] J. Duane Squires, "How a Baptist Confession Was Born," in *Baptist Leader,* Vol. 27, No. 1 (April, 1955), pp. 13-15.

[7] J. R. Graves, *Old Landmarkism: What Is It?* (Texarkana, Texas: Baptist Sunday School Committee, 1928), p. xiv.

Underlying Graves' ideas were two principles: (1) Baptists are distinct in being in a succession of true gospel churches; they therefore have the sole right to baptize and ordain. (2) The Lord's Supper is purely a local church ordinance for believers baptized by immersion. He looked to the church, not the Bible, for his authority. In this he identified "church" and "kingdom." Therefore, all passages in the Bible on the kingdom he applied to the local church.

From about 1880 the Landmarkists attacked the Southern Baptist Convention's mission board for its methods and control. This attack, especially in Arkansas, Texas, and Oklahoma, was bound up with personal rivalries between local leaders who had come under the influence of controversialists from Kentucky, Tennessee, and Georgia. This issue centered in the scriptural right of the individual churches to send out missionaries. The Landmarkists insisted on a "local mission" principle, and urged that representation in the associations and in the convention be on a church unit basis. The years from 1890 to 1930 were the time of the most intensive cultivation of the Landmark ideas. When the Southern Baptist Convention refused to conform to the Landmarkists' principle, the Baptist General Association was organized in 1905 in Texarkana. Membership was by church units. They insisted "that Landmark Baptist churches alone can establish historical connection with New Testament churches."[8] This Association published Graves' writings. Although the Southern Baptist Convention rejected the Landmarkists' attack on its missionary methods, Landmarkist ideas have exerted a significant influence upon many of the churches, causing them to remain aloof from ecumenical relationships which, they believe, threaten the autonomy of the local church.

[8] Duke K. McCall, ed., *What Is the Church?* (Nashville: Broadman Press, 1958), p. 143.

During the second half of the nineteenth century the local concept of the church was staunchly upheld and given wide circulation by Edward T. Hiscox's church manual, *The New Directory for Baptist Churches,* first published in 1859. It soon became the most popular manual on Baptist polity. By 1894 about 60,000 copies had been circulated in the United States, and translations of the book into at least seven languages had been made by American Baptist missionaries for use by the churches formed abroad under their influence. The independence of the local churches was upheld in the manual with vigor. A council of Baptist churches was regarded as an independent body within its own sphere of action; it was limited in its functioning to the matters delegated to it. The delegates, or messengers, who compose a council were in no sense representatives of the churches, for *"A Baptist Church cannot be represented in any other body;* nor can it transfer its authority or its functions to any persons either within, or external to itself, to act for it. . . ." It was stated in this manual that a Baptist church would violate its holy purpose and lose its identity as the body of Christ if it became a member of any other body.[9]

Although little was said in manuals on polity about the interdependence of the churches, a number of factors were influencing a shift in Baptist thinking about 1900. A growing concept of the world-wide mission of the church was emerging, stimulated largely by the first International Missionary Conference, held at Edinburgh in 1910. The increasing diversification of the ministry of the church in a complex industrial society forced consideration of the elimination of needless duplication and of cooperative effort in the interest of economy and efficiency. The rising social consciousness of the

[9] Edward T. Hiscox, *The New Directory for Baptist Churches* (Valley Forge: The Judson Press, 1894), pp. 63, 74-76, 318-320, 334.

churches, stimulated by Washington Gladden and Walter Rauschenbusch, drew the larger denominations into a common effort to meet the challenge of mushrooming cities and their shifting population.

A stirring toward unity, which we call the ecumenical movement, was being felt in American Protestantism. It was marked by the organization of the Federal Council of Churches of Christ in America in 1908. This was followed by the creation of the International Missionary Council in 1921 and the International Council on Religious Education in 1922. Meanwhile a World Conference on Faith and Order had emerged from the International Missionary Conference at Edinburgh in 1910. This led eventually to the provisional organization of the World Council of Churches in 1938, which was made permanent at Amsterdam in 1948. By 1950 the Federal Council of Churches and a number of other interdenominational agencies were merged into the National Council of Churches of Christ in the United States of America.

Against such a backdrop, we may now examine the actual practice of Baptist churches with references to this developing ecumenical movement.

ATTITUDE OF THE BAPTIST WORLD ALLIANCE

The awakening of a world-wide denominational consciousness of Baptists, which resulted in the organization of the Baptist World Alliance in London in 1905, was contemporary with the rising tide of interdenominational fellowship which was to broaden into the current ecumenical movement. Quite naturally, therefore, we should expect the Baptists to indicate an awareness of this growing trend, and to express some reaction to it. A review of the proceedings of the meetings of the Alliance held every five years following 1905 is disappointing in this respect. Occasional expressions of interest and concern were heard, but by and large, the Alliance took the attitude that it could not speak for its member bodies, which were conventions and conferences of Baptists in various parts of the world. Thus the Alliance skirted an issue which was controversial among many of its American constituents.

At the Second Congress of the Baptist World Alliance, in Philadelphia in 1911, a request from the newly created World Faith and Order Movement to send delegates to a conference on Christian unity was rejected on the grounds that only the affiliated bodies can act on such an invitation.[10] When the Third Congress met in Stockholm in 1923, Dr. E. Y. Mullins, president of Southern Baptist Theological Seminary in Louisville, Kentucky, presented "A Message of the Baptist World Alliance to the Baptist Brotherhood, to other Christian Brethren, and to the World." While affirming acceptance of the principle of Christian unity, he made it clear that Baptists cannot unite with others "in any centralized ecclesiastical organization wielding power over the individual conscience"; nor can they "accept the sacerdotal conception of the ministry which involves the priesthood of a class with special powers for transmitting grace."[11] At the Fifth Congress in Berlin in 1934, Dr. Gilbert Laws of England urged the Alliance to engage in a serious study of the New Testament concerning the church in order to compare Baptist polity with that of other denominations. He concluded, quite appropriately, by suggesting that Baptists could make their greatest contribution to Christian unity by developing greater unity among themselves.[12]

[10] *Baptist World Alliance, Recorded Proceedings for 1911,* p. 414. (The reports of subsequent meetings of the Baptist World Alliance are titled by the number of the meeting, *e.g., Third Baptist World Congress, Record of Proceedings, Official Report,* 1923.) For convenience this source will hereafter be referred to as BWA.

[11] BWA, *Proceedings for 1923,* p. 224.

[12] BWA, *Proceedings for 1934,* p. 175.

The 1937 Oxford and Edinburgh Conferences on *Life and Work* and *Faith and Order* placed new demands upon Baptists to take a positive position on the subject of Christian unity. Accordingly, the Executive Committee of the Baptist World Alliance named an international committee to consider and report concerning the results of the two ecumenical conferences. The chairman was the late Professor W. O. Carver of Southern Baptist Theological Seminary. Out of this study came a report to the Sixth Congress of the Alliance at Atlanta in 1939. The conclusions are sufficiently important to summarize here: (1) The immediate responsibility of the Alliance, it was agreed, was "to develop Baptist consciousness and cooperation" and to bear clearly its distinctive witness. (2) Some felt that the entrance of Baptists into the proposed World Council of Churches would be embarrassing because it would place them in association with churches which discount the convictions and practices of Baptists, and some of which actually persecute Baptists in state-church countries. (3) Others believed that Baptists could make a genuine contribution by entering the World Council of Churches with a clear understanding of the terms and conditions of membership. (4) It was clearly evident that "Cooperation in the World Council, or in any other form, cannot be purchased at the cost of breaches in our Baptist fellowship."[13]

When the Baptist World Alliance met in Copenhagen, Denmark, in 1947, the World Council of Churches was in its ninth year of provisional experience. A great world war had conditioned many to think soberly concerning a united Christian witness to a broken world. Against such a background Henry Cook of England pled with the Alliance to encourage their members to enter the World Council, which was to organize permanently in Amsterdam the following year. He

[13] BWA, *Proceedings for 1939*, pp. 126-134.

pointed out that in this relationship Baptists could make a contribution to other Christians without compromising their own convictions and witness. His point of view met with a vigorous protest from Dr. M. E. Dodd, of the Southern Baptist Convention. The Alliance took no action, since it followed a policy of leaving such matters of interchurch relationships to national unions of Baptists and since also the World Council of Churches provided membership for national church bodies only.[14] In later meetings of the Alliance this policy has been maintained. It is believed by many that the strong influence of the Southern Baptist Convention within the Alliance is a decisive factor in the reticence of the Alliance to express itself more vigorously on this topic, although British Baptists, the American Baptist Convention, and the two National Baptist Conventions (Negro) in the United States, as well as a few smaller bodies, are affiliated with the World Council of Churches.

THE AMERICAN BAPTIST CONVENTION
AND THE ECUMENICAL MOVEMENT

From the outset of the ecumenical movement in the United States, the American Baptist Convention has been officially identified with it. It became a charter member of the Federal Council of Churches of Christ in America in 1908. Four prominent Baptists served on the first Executive Committee of the Council: Dr. W. C. Bitting, of St. Louis; Dr. John B. Calvert and Dr. Howard B. Grose, of New York; and the Hon. H. Kirke Porter, of Pittsburgh. From 1913 to 1918, another Baptist, Professor Shailer Mathews, of the University of Chicago, served as president of the Federal Council of Churches.

From the outset, the financial contributions from participating denominations to the Federal Council were small, totaling but $12,000 out of a budget of nearly $250,000 in 1920. The

[14] BWA, *Proceedings for 1947,* pp. 56-59.

remainder was raised from interested individuals. In 1921, the Northern Baptist Convention (renamed American Baptist Convention in 1950), like other denominations, was asked for a larger appropriation; and an amount of $35,000 was included in the Convention's budget that year. But little more than $3,000 actually went to the Federal Council. In 1923-24, however, approximately $20,000 was paid by the Northern Baptist Convention toward its support; but the following year the amount dropped to less than $10,000. The actual budget item for 1925-26 was only $8,000. In 1929 the amount fell even lower, to $7,340, as over against $22,000 contributed by the Methodist Episcopal Church.[15]

The uphill struggle to win financial support for participation in the Federal Council of Churches was not alone due to the economic limitations of Baptists. It was due also to an opposition on the part of many to membership in the Council, which some regarded as socially radical and theologically liberal. When the Northern Baptist Convention met in San Francisco in 1932, Dr. W. B. Riley, leader of the fundamentalist wing, sought to delete the budgetary item of $7,500 for the Federal Council. His efforts were blocked by a compromise measure presented by Dr. J. W. Brougher, which reduced the amount to $3,750 and called for a special committee to look into the question of further relation of Northern Baptists to the Federal Council. The investigating committee recommended the following year that the Convention continue its affiliation with the Council, that appropriations be made upon a pro-rata basis, as they were for all other participating organizations in the Convention, and that representatives to the Council

[15] *Annual of the Northern Baptist Convention 1921,* pp. 248, 276; *Annual of the Northern Baptist Convention 1925,* pp. 45, 150; *Annual of the Northern Baptist Convention 1930,* pp. 248-250.

[16] *Annual of the Northern Baptist Convention 1932,* pp. 127-128; *Annual of the Northern Baptist Convention 1933,* pp. 112-118.

should be selected from among persons who possessed the largest confidence of the Convention as a whole.[16]

Part of the opposition was due to a fear that Baptists would lose their unique and historic witness by membership in the Federal Council. But there was also distaste among the more reactionary segment of the Convention for the social pronouncements of the Council. The relationship was aggravated in the 1940's by theological conflict between the fundamentalist and liberal wings of the Convention. In 1947, a Committee on Interdenominational Relationships was appointed by the Convention to study the relationship of the Northern Baptist Convention to the Federal Council of Churches and other interdenominational agencies with which it cooperated, and also to the World Council of Churches. Fundamentalist members of the Convention sought in vain to win support for membership in the newly organized National Association of Evangelicals, a rival organization to the Federal Council.[17]

The committee, which was chaired by Dr. Edwin H. Pruden of Washington, D. C., pointed out, in making its report at Milwaukee in 1948, the difficulties involved in devising means whereby the autonomy of the local church would be protected while at the same time maintaining the denomination's rightful place within cooperative Christianity.

The recommendations which were presented and adopted by the Convention are of sufficient importance to warrant a summary of them here: (1) The Convention agreed to recognize the right of every church to give or withhold support of the Federal Council. The total number of churches who wished to be recorded as opposed to participation in the work of the Council would be published by the Northern Baptist Convention in the year book without prejudicing their relationship to the Convention. (2) The appropriation of the Convention to the Federal Council should be raised

[17] *Year Book of the Northern Baptist Convention 1947,* p. 88.

from designated gifts for that purpose and from the distribu-
table undesignated funds of those churches which voiced no
objection to support of its work. (3) Churches should be re-
assured that the Convention's participation in the Federal
Council was not for the purpose of encouraging organic
church union. (4) Baptist representatives on the Executive
Committee of the Council should be nominated from all geographical areas of the Convention and their travel expenses
to meetings should be paid by the Convention.(5) The formation of the National Council of Churches, to embrace eight
interdenominational agencies including the Federal Council,
should be approved, and delegates to the new body should
be elected by the Convention. (6) The Convention should
maintain its present relations with the World Council of
Churches.[18]

In May, 1950, the Convention voted to become a constitu-
ent member of the National Council of the Churches of Christ
in the U.S.A., to be formed in December, 1950, in Cleveland.
In 1951 at Buffalo, a resolution was adopted which urged
American Baptist churches to work with other Christian
groups in the world, with national, state, and local councils
of churches, and with other Christian bodies, that the common
witness of the Christian faith might be strengthened. This
action was repeated at Denver in 1953, and in successive
years.[19] The passage of these resolutions was facilitated in
part by the absence of the fundamentalists, many of whom
had left the Convention since 1949, and in part by the growing sentiment in favor of cooperative Christianity.

American Baptist relationships to the world-wide ecumenical movement began in 1911 when the Northern Baptist Con-

[18] *Year Book of the Northern Baptist Convention 1948*, pp. 66-68.
[19] *Year Book of the American Baptist Convention, 1950*, pp. 187-188;
Year Book of the American Baptist Convention 1951, pp. 95-97; *Year
Book of the American Baptist Convention 1953*, pp. 73, 77.

vention voted to participate in the World Conference at Edinburgh in 1910. Dr. Cornelius Woelfkin, of New York, was the chairman of the Baptist Committee on Faith and Order. In 1920 its name was changed to the "Committee on Conference with Other Religious Bodies." It is possible that the move was made to avoid misunderstanding regarding the Baptists' point of view on interchurch conversations, for Baptists generally found themselves at variance with the ecclesiastical connotation which the term "faith and order" held for communions who were creedalists and whose ministry was according to ecclesiastical orders of the episcopal pattern.

The financial contributions of the Convention to the expenses of the conferences were exceedingly modest, ranging from under one hundred dollars to a thousand dollars in 1944-1945, and to ten thousand in 1953-1954. Delegates to conferences on faith and order attended at their own expense. They reflected the Baptist interest in unity of spirit and purpose rather than of organization. Through their conversations with representatives of other communions, American Baptists were preparing to take their place in the World Council of Churches. When the Second Assembly of the World Council met at Evanston, Illinois, in August, 1954, twelve delegates and an equal number of accredited visitors represented the American Baptist Convention. Interest of Baptists in ecumenical Christianity mounted as a result of the firsthand contact with the movement through the Evanston meeting and the months of study that had preceded it.

In June, 1960, the Convention was confronted at its meeting in Rochester by opposition to its continued membership in the National Council of Churches raised by representatives of the First Baptist Church of Wichita, Kansas. A demand was made that the Convention withdraw from membership on the grounds that the National Council was sympathetic to communism. The General Council of the Convention presented a resolution reaffirming its continued participation in the National Council of Churches and reaffirming the right of any local church to express dissent and withhold its financial support from the National Council and to be so listed in the official year book. After an orderly debate, the Convention approved the resolution of the General Council by a ratio of ten to one, thereby settling the issue of continued participation in cooperative Christianity.[20]

Since 1961, conversations have been authorized by the General Council with the Church of the Brethren, the Disciples of Christ, and Seventh Day Baptists. The most productive sessions have been held with the Church of the Brethren, a denomination of German Baptist heritage whose headquarters is located at Elgin, Illinois.

Since 1963, American Baptists have been represented by two observer-consultants at annual sessions of the Consultation on Church Union. This ecumenical effort began in 1962 when representatives of four denominations, the United Presbyterian Church in the U.S.A., the Protestant Episcopal Church, the United Church of Christ, and the Methodist Church met in Washington, D. C., to explore "the establishment of a united Church, truly catholic, truly reformed, and truly evangelical." This group of four denominations was joined in 1963 by the Disciples of Christ and the Evangelical United Brethren. When in 1965, the Consultation issued an invitation to denominations represented by observer-consultants to join as full participants in the attempt to formulate an outline of a plan of union, American Baptists debated the issue for nearly a year. Opinion was so divided that the General Council voted to continue the observer-consultant role on the grounds that full participation would fragment the Convention. To offset an impression that the Convention was with-

[20] J. C. Slemp, "Rochester, 1960," in *Missions*, Vol. 158, No. 6 (June, 1960), p. 24.

drawing from ecumenical involvement, the Council also voted to strengthen the current lines of participation of the Convention in the conciliar movement. It also brought into being a Commission on Christian Unity to be composed of persons qualified to engage the Convention in study of the next steps for American Baptists in the search for fuller Christian unity. When the Convention met in annual session at Kansas City in May, 1966, a resolution was adopted approving this action, but with a qualifying amendment that the Commission avoid taking steps which would violate or weaken the historic Baptist witness. This was illustrative of the ambivalence of American Baptists, and indeed of many other Free Churches, with respect to the nature of the Christian unity they sought.[21]

THE SOUTHERN BAPTIST CONVENTION AND THE ECUMENICAL MOVEMENT

Southern Baptists, like Northern Baptists, cooperated in the Home Missions Council (organized in 1908) and the Foreign Missions Conference of North America (organized in 1893) until 1950, when those bodies merged with the newly constituted National Council of Churches. Unlike Northern Baptists, however, they did not unite with the Federal Council of Churches of Christ in America or with the National Council of Churches into which it was absorbed in 1950. They refrained from taking such a step because they felt that membership would impair the autonomy of the local church. Also, by this time Southern Baptists objected to the limitations involved in comity agreements on mission fields. Moreover, they regarded the Council as being under the influence of theological liberals who "have magnified the implications of the gospel to the disparagement of the gospel itself." They also were critical of the social emphasis of the Council, which

[21] *Crusader,* Vol. 21, No. 6 (June, 1966), p. 2; see editorial in *The Christian Century,* Vol 83, No. 22 (June 1, 1966), pp. 705-706.

they regarded as promoting "class consciousness instead of social consciousness," and they resented its policy of pacifism with reference to war. Perhaps even more important in their decision not to identify themselves with the Federal Council or its successor was a belief that such a relationship would weaken their position on religious liberty. They argued that the parent bodies of a number of denominations within the council maintained an incomplete conception of religious liberty in Europe, where they still enjoyed the privileges of state churches, some of which persecuted minority groups.

Although Southern Baptists had delegates at the Faith and Order Conference at Edinburgh in 1937 and at the provisional conference on a World Council of Churches at Utrecht in 1938, they declined an invitation to membership in the World Council of Churches. Their decision was based upon a fear that such "a great over-all world ecclesiasticism would depend more on political pressure than upon spiritual power" and that "a close compact union of all non-Catholics would intensify the conflicts of Christendom" by arousing the Roman Catholics to an unprecedented rivalry. In addition, they claimed that membership in the World Council would threaten the autonomy of Free Churches and might jeopardize the witness of Baptists to believer's baptism and a regenerate church by a compromise with pedobaptist groups.[22]

When the Second Assembly of the World Council of Churches met at Evanston in 1954, however, there were a number of unofficial visitors from the Southern Baptist Convention present. Here and there in editorial comments on Evanston in Southern Baptist state convention papers there were glimmerings of a furtive desire on the part of some to

[22] W. R. White, *Baptist Distinctives* (Nashville: The Sunday School Board of the Southern Baptist Convocation, 1946), pp. 83-85. See also William W. Barnes, *The Southern Baptist Convention, 1845-1953* (Nashville: Broadman Press, 1954), chap. 18.

draw nearer to the ecumenical movement, although official reaction had not changed.

In closing this brief survey, it should be noted that some local Baptist churches in the Southern Baptist Convention have joined local federations of churches called by various names, while state conventions have declined on the grounds that Baptist polity precludes their uniting with any federation of churches. The same argument is used sometimes by local congregations within the American Baptist Convention to sustain objection to that body's affiliation with the National Council of Churches.

By 1964, the Southern Baptist Convention had grown in membership to more than ten and a half million. The churches, which numbered 33,388, were to be found in every state of the Union.[23] In spite of its size and numerical strength, diverse segments within the Convention's life prompt it to give chief attention to maintaining internal unity. One observer has pointed out that, "The disparity between Baptist climate in the more liberal southeastern states and in the very conservative southwestern states presents denominational leaders with an issue they deem far more pertinent than union with other Baptist bodies."[24] Among the diverse elements within the Convention are those who grieve over provincialism and disunity not only among Baptists but between Baptists and other Christians.

CONCLUSION

The strength of the spiritual impulse behind the ecumenical movement is evident from the degree of cooperation which Baptists give to it in spite of the grave obstacles which stand in the way, from the point of view both of polity and of theological and cultural differences between Baptists and

[23] *Annual of the Southern Baptist Convention, 1965,* p. 132.
[24] Hill and Torbet, *op. cit.,* p. 75.

other Christian communions. No doubt the degree of interest shown by Baptists in the movement is the more to be appreciated when one realizes that it has its birth in a deep spiritual solicitude on the part of many who voluntarily, and often without great encouragement, bear concern for the unity of the church of Jesus Christ. Certainly, the Baptist contribution to ecumenical thought and action is of greatest importance to all who welcome an emphasis upon that concept of unity which finds its expression in the fellowship of the Spirit rather than in the organizational structure and uniformity of creed and worship.

This summary of the Baptist approach to Christian unity points up the fundamental dilemma of the Free Churches—how to balance an essentially exclusive view of the church gathered in congregations of Christians committed to maintaining the pristine life and faith which characterized the New Testament witness with an inclusive view of the universal church which embraces divergent concepts of the nature of the church and its relationship to culture. Perhaps in no branch of Christianity are the divisive effects of the Protestant Reformation so evident as in the Free Churches, for they have virtually made separation an essential to the recovery of the pure church. Accordingly, this branch of the Christian family faces the deepest soul searching in taking seriously the restoration of unity to a fragmented Christianity. They must ask whether this unity is to lead to eventual corporate union, and whether this goal can be achieved without threatening their hard-won struggle to achieve religious liberty. For many of them, a unity which fails to make room for diversity is a contradiction of the biblical meaning of freedom in Christ.

Chapter 6

A COMMITTED APPROACH
TO CHRISTIAN UNITY

WHEN THE SPRINGFIELD PRESBYTERY met at Cane Ridge, center of the Great Western Revival, to decree its own dissolution on June 28, 1804, it proclaimed this action in a brief document called "The Last Will and Testament of the Springfield Presbytery." The document began with the words:

> We *will* that this body die, be dissolved, and sink into union with the Body of Christ at large; for there is but one Body, and one Spirit, even as we are called in one hope of our calling.[1]

In a way, this statement and the action which accompanied it are symbolic of the importance of Christian unity in the Disciples' tradition.

Those historic words summarized five Presbyterian ministers' impatience with the stern doctrine of election held by Old School Presbyterians and their protest against the use of the Westminster Confession as a standard of doctrine. They believed that these requirements stood in the way of the

[1] Winfred Ernest Garrison and Alfred T. DeGroot, *The Disciples of Christ: A History* (St. Louis: The Bethany Press, 1948), p. 109.

larger Christian fellowship which they had come to experience in the evangelical revivals of their day. In 1803 they had withdrawn from the Synod of Kentucky to organize an independent presbytery. Nine months later they disbanded this presbytery and organized the "Christian Church," a church without sectarian distinctives or denominated labels. This movement, led by Barton W. Stone, was soon strengthened by a second under the leadership of Thomas Campbell who had withdrawn in 1809 from the Seceder branch of the Presbyterian Church after he had been disciplined for his attacks upon what he regarded as the divisiveness of his denomination. These attacks were embodied in 1807 in a now famous document entitled *Declaration and Address.* In the same year, he had organized the Christian Association of Washington (Pa.), which was non-creedal and lacked the jurisdictional authority of synods and presbyteries over local congregations. His aim was to restore primitive Christianity in order to achieve the "unity, peace and purity" of the church.

Campbell was joined by his son, Alexander, who also had broken with Seceder Presbyterians a few months earlier while a student in Glasgow. Their adoption of the immersion of believers in preference to baptism of infants brought them into sympathy with the Baptists. In 1813 the Christian Association, which had become a local church, applied for admission to the Redstone Baptist Association in Pennsylvania. The connection with the Baptists continued until underlying differences culminated in a complete separation of Baptists and Disciples by 1830.

In 1832, the Christians (followers of Stone) and Disciples (followers of the Campbells) united. The term "Christian" became the preferred name although the term "Disciples of Christ," was used in census reports and the like. This union produced some 20,000 to 30,000 members. By 1849, there emerged the first national convention, the annual meeting of the American Christian Missionary Society. By 1850 the number of Disciples had grown to about 118,000.[2] While they went through the Civil War without division over the slavery question, controversy over "innovations" (such as missionary societies and instrumental music) led to some losses as proponents and opponents went their separate ways. By 1906 the Federal Religious Census listed two separate groups, the Disciples of Christ and the Churches of Christ. What had begun as a protest against denominational divisions within Christianity had itself become a denomination. But it never lost its zeal for recovering the wholeness of the church.

This chapter will examine the ways by which the Disciples have developed this ecumenical concern, especially in relation to the changing trends of the twentieth century. Their reactions have been set alongside those of the Baptists, since both groups, although differing in several respects, have held a common core of beliefs and concerns which has drawn them together at times in their history. In spite of their differences, Baptists and Disciples represent, each in their own way, the manner in which free churches have responded to the growing quest for more visible Christian unity.

PRINCIPLES AND MOTIVATIONS OF DISCIPLES

Two basic ideas were from the beginning in the minds of the founders of the Disciples of Christ. One was the reunion of all Christians. The other was the restoration of the essentials of primitive Christianity. Both the followers of Barton W. Stone and the adherents of Alexander Campbell conceived of restoration as a means of promoting unity among Christians.

Predominantly a rural people through the nineteenth century, the Disciples maintained a strong sense of individualism both in personal Christian experience and in the independence

[2] *Ibid.,* pp. 16-19.

of the local congregations. Yet, unlike the Baptists, who allowed their congregationalism to overshadow the larger concept of the church held by their forebears, the Disciples held to the ecumenical ideal. For them, however, Christian unity was more a spiritual vision than an ecclesiastical reality. So long as they brought to the New Testament a literalism of interpretation and insisted upon the right and duty of every Christian to make a direct appeal to the Scriptures, they stressed the autonomy of each local church "as against any representative body of wider scope having delegated authority." Indeed, "the promotion of an actually united church does not appear as a major objective."[3]

It was not until the twentieth century that fresh impetus and a new perspective created among Disciples a renaissance of ecumenical thought. A number of elements contributed to this new direction in their mission to be a unifying church. One was the social gospel movement which drew many thoughtful Christians, especially in the developing urban centers of the nation, to add to their understanding of evangelism a concern to change the social order so as to create a Christian environment in which new converts might be nurtured and find economic, social, and political justice. This passion for social reform stimulated interdenominational cooperation and so contributed to the concern for the unity of the church. A second element was the new approach to the Bible stimulated by biblical scholars who were challenging the inerrancy of the text and the validity of literalistic interpretation which failed at points to take into account the literary forms and thought patterns of the biblical writers. A third element was the gradual urbanization of segments of the Disciples' Brotherhood. A fourth was the growing influence of the ecumenical movement which had come to prominence in the United States.

[3] *Ibid.,* p. 110.

A serious effort to achieve union with the Baptists began in 1910 and culminated in 1946 when the Disciples unanimously approved a resolution for union with the Northern Baptist Convention. Conferences were held in 1947-1948, but the efforts failed because of opposition of some Baptists to the Disciples' viewpoint regarding baptism as a part of the conversion process.[4] In the years that followed, the Disciples sought to fulfill their functions as a uniting church on a wider scale than unilateral talks with like-minded communions permitted. In a sense, they were risking their ideal of primitive Christianity in order to achieve the ecumenical goal. This had led them into full participation in the Consultation on Church Union—an enterprise of major Protestant denominations in quest of a new church which would reduce the division within American Protestantism. The Disciples represented in the Consultation a free church that was willing to explore union with more centralized churches having creeds, bishops, and infant baptism. In turn the Disciples have brought to the Consultation a strong witness to the Free Church viewpoint regarding diversity within unity, believer's baptism, and the subordination of form to the life of the Spirit.

In substantiation of their new position in the search for unity, the newer historians among the Disciples have pointed out that a specific polity is not to be found in the primitive church, as once believed by Disciples and many other communions. This viewpoint, which allows a broader concept of the church while still following the insights of the New Testament Christianity has prompted a reevaluation by Disciples of their original goal to restore primitive church life. Questions like this are being asked: What is it that should be restored? Were the founding fathers mistaken in their effort

[4] *Ibid.*, pp. 557 f. and Franklin E. Rector, "Behind the Breakdown of Baptist-Disciple Conversations on Unity," in *Foundations*, Vol. 4, No. 2 (April, 1961), pp. 120-137.

to restore some practices which were not really a part of the primitive church, but rather an assumption of what it seemed to be through the eyes of literalists and legalists?

Illustrative of this trend is the position of Dr. Winfred E. Garrison, notable church historian, who controverted the thesis of the Campbells, Scott, and Stone "that there was a divinely authorized uniform plan for the organization of the church" clearly set forth in the New Testament to be followed in their proposed "restoration" of primitive Christianity. He insisted that while there is indication of a graduated scale of clergy, there is none which has episcopal, synodical, or any other form of control over local congregations. He concluded that the Protestant reformers should have gone all the way back to the primitive Christian era—behind the mistaken interpretation of both literalists and advocates of a totalitarian Catholicism.[5]

UPDATING THE CHURCH

The Disciples entered the twentieth century with 1,120,000 members. Changes in the religious world of the new century widened rifts among them. As we have seen, the increasing stress on social problems of applied Christianity and a wider acceptance of the "new view" of the Bible based upon historical and textual criticism had broadened the views of some Disciples and aroused resentment and resistance among others. The trend from a loosely conceived Brotherhood of autonomous churches to a cooperation through societies and conventions led to the withdrawal in 1906 of a group who styled themselves "Churches of Christ." Fundamentalist in doctrine and conservative in social outlook, this splinter group numbered less than a half million by 1926 and were most numerous in Texas, Arkansas, and Tennessee.[6]

[5] Garrison and DeGroot, op. cit., pp. 25, 38.
[6] Ibid., pp. 402-405.

The new sense of ethical and social responsibility among the major body of Disciples was reflected by their charter membership in the Federal Council in 1908 and in the new liberalism expressed by the *Christian Century,* a publication bought by Charles Clayton Morrison, a notable Disciple journalist, in 1908, and destined to become the twentieth-century voice of liberal Protestantism.

The task of restructuring the Brotherhood into an effective denominational assembly began in 1958. It was the result of a long period of ecclesiastical evolution. The right to organize churches into an association or convention was hard won. Walter Scott, one of the early founders, had not been able 'n find authorization for such organization in the New Testament. By 1869, however, societies of individuals were trans-termed by the Louisville Plan into a single church-centered corporation known as the General Missionary Convention. The Plan did not receive financial support, so it was abandoned in 1874. The General Christian Missionary Convention did not, however, go out of existence. Instead, it revised its constitution in 1881 to include the traditional membership basis of individual rather than church support. In the ensuing years, the missionary societies were engaged in competition and frequent conflict. Finally, in 1912 at Louisville, a proposal was adopted by the Brotherhood to organize on a delegate basis a general convention of churches—not of societies, as some wanted. The plan did not succeed, however. When, in 1917 the new convention was enlarged at Kansas City to become the International Convention of Disciples of Christ, the Assembly was once again restored as a mass meeting. In 1920 six major agencies were merged into the United Missionary Society. In this form they became affiliated in 1922 with the Convention. Thus the instruments of mission were more closely related to the churches.

The task of restructuring this loosely organized Convention

into a deliberative assembly of delegates on a representative principle was entrusted in 1960 to a Commission on Brotherhood Restructure. The task of the Commission of 130 persons was to determine how 8,000 churches could act cooperatively in evangelism, missions, education, stewardship, benevolence, and social action. The traditional distrust of ecclesiasticism and church organization had sufficiently dissipated to allow the Commission to view objectively the institutional life of Disciples. The development of denominational scholars and participation in the ecumenical movement had led them, according to one observer, to a more tolerant view of centralized churchmanship which would avoid the extremes of anarchy and authoritarianism.[7]

Ronald E. Osborn, historian and dean of Christian Theological Seminary in Indianapolis, Indiana, described Disciples of the past two generations as having quietly dropped or having openly repudiated "pattern-restorationism" in favor of a recognition of the dynamic nature of the early church, the variety of early Christian practice, and the need to do some ecclesiastical restructuring for the present day. He defined the task of the Commission in terms of helping "the congregation to see its responsibility toward the church of Christ at large and its obligation to share both in decision-making and in burden-bearing."[8]

While new attitudes toward ecclesiastical structures and the need for updating the Brotherhood were coming to the fore, the traditional restorationist idealism was still intact. This included a strong emphasis upon the primacy of Christian experience over doctrinal formulations, a fundamental reliance upon the Bible (although with a more liberal atti-

[7] C. E. Lemmon, "The Time Is at Hand," in *Mid-Stream*, Vol. 2, No. 2 (December, 1962), pp. 14-18.

[8] Ronald E. Osborn, "The Structure of Cooperation," *ibid.*, pp. 29, 48.

tude), a firm insistence that structure follows function and should never be allowed to obstruct the Christian's consciousness of the lordship of Christ.[9]

By 1963 the Commission had outlined the nature of the structure that it was seeking: (1) It was to be rooted in Christ's servant ministry made known through the Scriptures. (2) It was to be comprehensive in ministry and mission. (3) It was to be the means by which congregations could fulfill their ministries. (4) It was to be a means by which the local churches were to be responsibly interrelated. (5) It was to manifest both unity and diversity. (6) It was to be ecumenical in its purpose and scope. (7) It was to be faithful in stewardship. In total, it was to transform a loose Brotherhood of Disciples into the Christian Church, a purpose which was tested by a straw vote in 1963.[10]

At the fourth meeting of the Commission in 1965 a recommendation to the Brotherhood was formulated to move the Disciples structurally toward the organization of the Christian Church (Disciples of Christ). The plan of conventions of "voting representatives" called for local congregations to be associated together in "regions." Each congregation would be entitled to name voting representatives to compose a biennial regional assembly. Local congregations and regions would elect representatives to constitute a general assembly for the whole church, to meet biennially.[11] It was to be put to a vote of the International Convention in the fall of 1968.

This proposal was met by opposition from some quarters. The Commission explained that the proposed delegate con-

[9] "Program, Proceedings and Discussions of the Commission on Brotherhood Restructure," in *Mid-Stream*, Vol. 3, No. 1 (September, 1963), pp. 18, 22.

[10] "The Nature of the Structure Our Brotherhood Seeks," in *Mid-Stream*, Vol. 4, No. 1 (Fall, 1964), pp. 24-27.

[11] "A Preliminary Proposal on Design," in *Mid-Stream*, Vol. 5, No. 1 (Fall, 1965), pp. 96-97.

ventions of the Christian Church would increase the ability of Disciples to hear and to understand each other and so increase "that kind of knowledge which is properly the content of Christian conscience." It was further explained that delegate conventions were also to provide "an honest record of the voice of the Church to which we may harken." The shift, in effect, was to be "from the society concept to the churchly concept" of structures for mission. Behind this concept was the ecumenical ideal basic to the purpose of Disciples. Through the churchly concept, the congregations were to recognize a wider ministry—in the state, nation, and world —as participants in the church of Christ in which each local congregation is a part of the larger whole.[12]

It should be observed in passing that there has been within the ranks of the Disciples some public opposition to restructure and that most of the fears expressed involve an attack on the Consultation on Church Union. Nevertheless, these attacks represent only a small portion of the cooperative leadership, and most of the persons who have participated in them have indicated that they will follow the general decision when it is made. Much more strident opposition comes from the "independent churches" associated with the North American Christian Convention. While no formal schism has occurred, most of these churches and the agencies they support refuse to apply to themselves the title "Disciples of Christ." They call themselves Christian Churches (as most Disciples do too).[13]

[12] W. B. Blakemore, "Freedom, Authority and Responsibility in the Church," *ibid.*, pp. 65-67.

[13] The author is indebted to Dean Ronald E. Osborn, church historian and Disciples churchman, for these observations. An examination of the editorial pages of the *Christian Standard* for the 1960's will provide a sample of the "independent" attacks on restructure and the Consultation on Church Union.

47482

WHAT DISCIPLES ENVISION FOR THE FUTURE

The goal of the Disciples is the restoration of primitive Christianity with its basic unity of the church. Dr. Alfred T. DeGroot, church historian and interpreter of the Disciples, has observed that the "restoration principle" stunts the spiritual development of the church when it is conceived in terms of a "legalistic primitivism." Its glory and contribution, however, can be seen "when it is defined in essentially spiritual terms." The Disciples, he believes, have been hampered "by those ultraconservative elements which would reduce Christianity to mechanisms and verbalisms." It is essential, therefore, that they "re-examine their heritage and restore the true essentials of their faith."[14]

The future of the Disciples' witness is dependent, then, upon the recognition of six principles: (1) The aims or purposes of the church should determine the means. (2) The unity already present in the church should be affirmed, cultivated, and enlarged. (3) The optimism and expectancy of the primitive church should be recaptured. (4) The concept of freedom should be made the overarching ideal for the church. (5) The church should discover what is essential to worship and life as discerned by sincere Christians. (6) A conquering spiritual life should be recaptured.[15]

The achievement of this restorationist goal by the Disciples is to be within an ecumenical context. Since 1963 the Disciples' participation in the Consultation of Church Union has drawn them into the center of American ecumenism. They stand in the forefront of the free churches in this respect, bringing to the Protestant quest for more visible unity of Christians the enrichment of their tradition.

[14] Alfred T. DeGroot, *The Restoration Principle* (St. Louis: The Bethany Press, 1960), pp. 7-8, 164.
[15] *Ibid.*, pp. 169-185.

One of the ablest exponents of the newer and broader involvement of Disciples is Dean Ronald E. Osborn, whose book *A Church for These Times* interprets the objectives of the Consultation on Church Union which are the creation of a church truly evangelical, truly reformed, and truly catholic. In the spirit of a free churchman, he sees the vitality of the church deriving "not from the forms of its life but from its continuing encounter with the Holy Spirit."[16] He calls upon the church to give the Bible a central place in determining its liturgy, its preaching, its educational program, and its style of life. It is the primary instrument of the Holy Spirit in the guidance of the church.[17]

Catholicity, he believes, makes for the wholeness of the church, not as tests but as affirmations of praise and continuity with all generations of the faithful, and its communion with the risen Lord. Reflecting the new stance of Disciples, he recognizes the place of creeds in the life of a reunited church, not as tests, but as affirmations of praise and confession. He does not see a threat to free churchmen in the Consultation's concept of ministry ordered about a pastoral (not administrative) bishop. The catholicity of the church is to be a manifestation of Christ's lordship and a condition of mission. The wholeness of the church is needed "not to exercise power but to manifest oneness, to overcome the irrelevance of denominational distinctions in the face of the world's need."[18]

Dr. Winfred E. Garrison, a leading churchman among the Disciples and a long-time advocate of reducing divisions within Protestantism, outlined in 1957 eight characteristics which a united church should have: (1) mutual love between

[16] Ronald E. Osborn, *A Church for These Times* (Nashville: Abingdon Press, 1965), p. 69.

[17] *Ibid.*, pp. 86-97.

[18] *Ibid.*, pp. 118-139, 156-157.

members, (2) an interchangeable membership, (3) an interchangeable ministry, (4) varieties of organization and structure existing independently but harmoniously within the united church, (5) no creedal or doctrinal test, (6) similar liberty in the use and interpretation of the sacraments, (7) equal freedom for congregations in the use of various forms of worship, (8) agencies of cooperation.[19] The extent to which these characteristics have been incorporated into the Consultation's Principles of Church Union and Guidelines for Structure[20] indicates the degree of influence which Disciples have had in this significant quest of nine major denominations for greater Christian unity in a revolutionary age.

The Disciples' approach to the achievement of Christian unity demonstrates how a Free Church can embrace creatively both the renewal of the church and the recovery of its essential unity. They believe that the achievement of both goals is possible within a basic loyalty to the essentials of New Testament Christianity broadly applied in the new context of the twentieth century.

[19] Winfred E. Garrison, *The Quest and Character of a United Church* (Nashville: Abingdon Press, 1957), pp. 223-227.

[20] For the text see, *Consultation on Church Union 1967*, pp. 19-73.

Chapter 7

POINTERS TO A RESOLUTION
OF THE FREE CHURCH DILEMMA

THUS FAR THE RISE of the Free Church tradition and its essential tenets, with particular emphasis upon the concern within this tradition for Christian unity, has been described. For illustration, the attempts of two Free Churches, the Baptists and the Disciples of Christ, to deal with the ecumenical ideal and particularly the ecumenical movement of the twentieth century have been compared.

In the light of this discussion, what is the prospect for a resolution of the Free Church dilemma? Does it lie in a perpetuation of the Free Churches in at least a partial separation from other communions in order to identify and preserve their historic distinctives? Or does it lie in the halfway house of interdenominational cooperation? At the present time, only a segment of the Free Church wing of Protestantism is identified with the National Council of Churches and the World Council. Another segment is identified with the National Association of Evangelicals. Still another is composed of denominational groupings which remain in isolation from other churches. An indication of this isolationism was evident in the Conference on the Concept of the Believer's Church held in July, 1967, at Louisville, Kentucky. It brought together more than twenty different communions—Brethren, Friends, Church of God, Mennonite, Baptist, and the like. The general comment among the delegates was: "It is a miracle that we are together." The trend of the papers and discussion centered in a strong conviction that by their concept of the believer's church, which they held in common, they were identified with primitive Christianity. Most of the groups present were not in the conciliar movement and were not prone to organize a federation of their own.

Such a sectarian trait creates for the Free Churches a major problem. How can they relate their desire to restore primitive Christianity, according to the standard they have found in the New Testament, to the current quest of other Christians for more visible unity? The issue raises the question whether it is possible for Free Churches to participate in mergers with other communions of different polity and concepts of worship and mission without losing the essential of their Free Church witness. For many Free Churches the question has never been considered since they have not yet been induced to unite with Christians of like polity and faith. For them the principle of restorationism leaves little room for ecumenical considerations.

REFORMATION AND CATHOLICITY

Gustav Aulén, Swedish theologian, in a book entitled *Reformation and Catholicity*, has developed the thesis that the Reformers were interested in maintaining the catholicity of the church. They had not intended to create "a new church." They wanted only to restore the church to its apostolic prototype. Consequently, they regarded the reformed churches which were the product of their efforts as a continuation of the Apostolic Church which the early creeds described as "one, holy, and catholic." Indeed, most of the Reformers did not understand "justification by faith" in purely individualistic or subjective terms, but as *"that continuing redemptive activity which the living Christ, present and active in the Word and the Sacraments, carries on in and through his church."*[1]

Catholicity for the radical reformers, especially for those of the Puritan and Anabaptist traditions, was to be defined not in geographical terms but in qualitative ones. They rejected the "Constantinian order" of Christendom for the conventicles of the faithful gathered by the Holy Spirit. Their consequent emphasis upon a distinctive style of life and an uncompromising rejection of the standards of the world led them to interpret Christian unity in spiritual terms rather than in organizational terms which might involve them again in compromise with a religious but worldly society. For them, freedom from entangling alliances with both the state and the "corrupt" state church was a fundamental principle to be obeyed and preserved at great sacrifice.

The worth of this principle is being viewed sympathetically by reform elements within the Roman Catholic Church. Michael Novak, Catholic lay theologian, sees the Anabaptists as the "full-way" reformers whose notion of the church as a rejection of the Constantinian order resembled the Franciscans and seventeenth-century pietists in their common effort to restore the early form of Christianity.[2] The main differences between the Catholic Franciscan orders and the Anabaptists was, according to his interpretation, that the former saw themselves "as living a special form of life within a larger religious

---

[1] Gustaf Aulén, *Reformation and Catholicity* (Philadelphia: Fortress Press, 1961), p. 60.

[2] Michael Novak, "The Free Churches and the Roman Church," in *Journal of Ecumenical Studies*, Vol. 2, No. 3 (1965), pp. 429-432.

community," whereas the latter regarded the church as co-
terminous with their own brotherhood.

Novak enumerates two major contributions of the Anabaptists to world history: (1) their break with the Constantinian
order; (2) their adoption of a congregational polity whereby
a strict discipline could be maintained through "a vigorous
congregational life." This was encouraged by an explicit covenant or pledge and by the Holy Spirit's teaching through consensus, i.e., through the conscience of the individual and of
the community, and by the discipline of free and honest discussion. He concludes that the issue between the Free
Churches and Roman Catholics is not individualism versus a
disciplined community, but how that discipline is to be attained. Both groups, he advises, can learn from each other's
strengths and weaknesses, even as they move from opposite
directions toward a common ground.[3]

According to Ernest A. Payne, a leading Free Church ecumenist who served many years as general secretary of the
Baptist Union of Great Britain and Ireland and as vice chairman of the Central Committee of the World Council of
Churches, the common ground which free churchmen have
with the Reformation is their protest against the authoritarian
episcopal method of maintaining the discipline of the church.
He explained that the Free Churches, in common with most of
the Lutheran and all of the continental Reformed Churches,
had broken with the episcopal order on three grounds: (1)
The fact that the New Testament uses the Greek words *pres-
byteros* (presbyter), and *episcopos* (bishop) interchangeably,
and so does not teach a threefold order of ministry. (2) The
theological argument that such an authoritarian ministry is
out of keeping with the spirit and letter of the New Testament.
The very notion of episcopacy, he argues, is an artificial theory

[3] *Ibid.*, p. 437.

of how the grace of God and the work of the Holy Spirit is continued in the church. The proper succession, he explains, should be that of insight and love, not of office. (3) The historical argument of the Free Churches' unhappy experiences with episcopacy, and their conviction that the episcopacy had not succeeded in maintaining "either the unity of the Church, the continuity of the Church, or the purity of its doctrine." Although admitting the historic Free Church position regarding the episcopacy, Payne points out that some free churchmen, like Richard Baxter of the seventeenth century, Robert Hall of the eighteenth century, and P. T. Forsyth of the early twentieth century, have expressed a willingness to look sympathetically on a kind of episcopal order of ministry characteristic of the second and third centuries. This was pastoral in function, without the administrative authority and ecclesiastical power that developed in later centuries.[4]

As an ecumenical free churchman, Payne argues that no Christian dare surrender the concept of catholicity, for the word "catholic" expresses the biblical view of the extension of the church throughout the world; it signifies the wholeness of the Christian faith which is indispensable to the fullness of the gospel; it indicates the inclusive character of the Christian fellowship; and it expresses the fullness of healing which the church has to bring to all of the ills and sins of mankind. He reminds the Free Churches that catholicity was a part of their heritage, for the Anabaptists "not only expounded the Apostles' Creed" (which affirms the catholicity of the church); "they put it into verse for congregational singing."[5] Thus, if "they put it into verse for congregational singing."[5] Thus, he affirms catholicity for the Free Churches.

[4] Ernest A. Payne, *Free Churchmen, Unrepentant and Repentant* (London: The Carey Kingsgate Press, Ltd., 1965), pp. 48-55.

[5] An address by Ernest A. Payne, "I Believe in the Holy Catholic Church," *The Baptist Quarterly*, Vol. 20, No. 4 (October, 1963), pp. 108-109.

ISSUES WHICH FREE CHURCHES MUST FACE

If the Free Churches are to take their place in the current ecumenical movement and not reject or ignore the catholicity of the church, they will need to face frankly some basic issues which have been and, for many, continue to be obstacles to full Christian unity.

1. *First is the issue created by the assumption of many free churchmen that Christian unity is invisible and that it cannot be made visible without sacrificing the freedom of the individual conscience to give primary allegiance to Jesus Christ.* Behind this assumption is a long history of protest against the "Constantinian order" of Christianity which gave to medieval Europe an institutionalized form of Christendom in which state and church were united and the freedom to reform and renew the life of the church was limited by the expedient concerns of the state and politically-minded church leaders. Because the main instrument within the church for its discipline of its inner life was the bishop's office, the episcopacy came under attack, with particular emphasis upon the papal claims of supremacy and infallibility.

2. *Still another issue is the nature of Christian unity itself.* The Free Churches, out of a fear of a coerced uniformity, whether creedal or structural, have defined unity in spiritual terms by which they have meant that the bonds which unite Christians are not organizationally discerned but are known to God. The closest approximation then of the true Bride of Christ is the congregation whose membership is composed only of those who have personally responded to the gospel by an act of commitment, often associated with a conversion experience. Beyond this reality of Christian fellowship in a common faith and worship, there is no church. The local congregations may cooperate in various ways, but the instrument of cooperation is not recognized as being the church.

This distinction made by the Free Churches between the church invisible and universal and a church visible and local cannot be supported by the New Testament. The writers of the Scriptures did not talk about a unity which has no clear expression. While the spiritual nature of the church is clearly taught, it is expressed in the Hebrew imagery of the body, which incorporates the spirit and the flesh in a single reality. Hence, the church has a visible, material expression of its oneness in Christ. This truth was reflected in the statement on Christian unity set forth by the North American Conference on Faith and Order at Oberlin, Ohio, in 1957: "The unity we envisage will be a unity which gives visible expression to the fact that we do belong to the one household of God."[6] The statement further explains that the gospel, by its reconciling nature, creates Christian unity because it proclaims that: (1) God has created man for unity in the bonds of love for him and for his neighbor. (2) God has restored the broken unity of mankind in Jesus Christ. (3) God renews the church for its mission. The statement goes on to say, "The individual Christian has membership in the Church Universal through the local congregation" and, "the organized life of the congregation is a testing ground of ecumenicity."[7] It is in the congregation that the nature of the whole church of Christ is made most visible.

The New Delhi Statement on Unity of the Third Assembly of the World Council of Churches (1961) described the church in similar terms, as "One fully committed fellowship, united with the whole Christian fellowship in all places and all ages," breaking the one bread and joining in common prayer, and having a corporate life with ministry and members accepted by all and so united that "all can act and speak

[6] Paul S. Minear, ed., *The Nature of the Unity We Seek* (St. Louis: The Bethany Press, 1958), p. 183.

[7] *Ibid.*, pp. 176-180, 208, 213.

together as occasion requires for the tasks to which God calls his people."[8] This is a unity that is visible, for mission to the world, although it may not be encompassed within a single comprehensive organization.

Forrest L. Knapp, general secretary of the Massachusetts Council of Churches, has pointed out that interdenominational cooperation through councils of churches can be either a dead-end street or a highway to unity. He cites four reasons why such cooperation may become a dead-end street: (1) It may express just enough unity to salve consciences. (2) It may confirm and strengthen denominations in their independence. (3) It may be comparatively superficial. (4) Denominations may decline to use their interchurch councils for advancement to full unity.[9]

Then he explains how councils of churches can enable interchurch cooperation to become a highway to unity: (1) A council can stir a dissatisfaction with present disunity and give vision for greater unity. (2) It can teach the lessons to be learned from the history of division and unity. (3) It can help overcome the obstacles to unity. (4) It can lead member churches toward unity through deepened fellowship and cooperation and identification with the larger Christian community and thence with the universal Church of Christ. (5) It may promote and guide concrete steps toward specific unions of churches. (6) It may provide the part-way house to unity by gradually increasing unity through cooperation until the full measure of desired unity is achieved.[10]

If the essence of the Free Church position is the imperative that the church be truly the body of Christ, remaining un-

[8] Forrest L. Knapp, *Church Cooperation: Dead-End Street or Highway to Unity?* (Garden City, N. Y.: Doubleday & Company, Inc., 1966), pp. 136, 145.

[9] *Ibid.,* pp. 214-220.

[10] *Ibid.,* pp. 221-239.

fettered by lesser loyalties for its primary allegiance to Jesus Christ its Head with respect to its message, its mandate to mission, its style of life, and its worship, then the Free Churches should be as concerned as other Christians for a greater manifestation of this witness to the world of our time. To set aside frankly the sectarianism that has characterized so many of the Free Churches and to join hands with all other Christians who are earnestly seeking the reintegration and renewal of the body of Christ is not to lose the essence of the Free Church idea but to invest it in the life of the whole body.

Where plans of union may be an option, the Free Churches, like other Christian communions, may do well to follow the principles recommended at Oberlin: (1) A plan of union must find some kind of visible expression. (2) It must seek to represent the faith of the Una Sancta (the Whole Church). (3) It must make clear that the nature of the church and the ministry cannot be dissociated from the faith of the whole church. (4) It must clarify how apostolicity is related to historical continuity. (5) It should reflect true repentance for disunity. (6) It must recognize the effect of social and cultural factors in the development of churches.[11]

To each of these principles, the Free Churches can bring their best insights. In nearly every one of these Churches there is already some recognition, if not acceptance, of one or more of these principles. For example, there is a common depository of the faith of the whole church expressed in the historic creeds of the early church, in the hymns shared in common with other Christians, in a common Bible, and in a vast body of Christian teaching which has come down from the great Bible teachers and theologians of the centuries. Then, too, the Free Churches can bring to the fourth principle their understanding of the meaning of apostolicity and the historical

[11] Minear, *op. cit.*, pp. 236-238.

continuity of a witnessing people. It may well be that they may find more agreement with their position from other Christians than would have been true a half century ago. As the "Constantinian order" of Christendom has crumbled in the face of rival powers—totalitarian statism, religious indifferentism, and secularization of values—state churches in Europe have been seeking freedom from political ties that hamper their renewal for effective mission. Even the Roman Catholic Church, as Michael Novak has indicated, is moving toward the Protestant reform position in its own renewal.

3. *Another issue for some Free Churches derives from their understanding of the meaning of baptism.* Unfortunately, it is not always referred to in this way, because some erroneously place the stress on the method of baptizing rather than on who is baptized. The latter consideration involves, of course, the meaning of the sacrament.

On the one hand are the confirmed anti-paedobaptists who are convinced that the baptism of persons who consciously and voluntarily express their faith in Jesus Christ is alone scriptural, and that baptism of infants is unscriptural and therefore to be rejected. These who acknowledge only believer's baptism are equally convinced that the church consists only of the converted. On the other hand are those who believe that an expression of faith commits not only oneself but also one's children to an act of initiation and training in the faith, to be followed by confirmation on the basis of a personal act of the will. These accept infant baptism as well as believer's baptism.

A. Gilmore, a younger British Baptist theologian, has expressed the viewpoint that such an issue can be resolved only when the discussion focuses upon the nature of the church in an ecumenical manner. He outlines a basic approach as follows: (1) What do we mean by faith, which all Christians relate to baptism? Is it an objective fact or a subjective experience? (2) What is the relationship between faith and sacraments, between the spiritual and the material? (3) What is the relationship between baptism and church membership? (4) What about rebaptism? What does it imply? (5) What is the place of children in the covenant among those who baptize infants? (6) What do the advocates of believer's baptism mean by the dedication of children?[12]

A notable Congregationalist theologian, P. T. Forsyth, argued in 1917 that many in the Free Churches have been all too reticent to recognize their sacramental heritage. By this he meant that they have feared that men might believe that God *does* something in the sacraments. Disavowing this, they insisted that nothing happens in baptism. Yet they require its observance, without always providing a theological justification for the sacraments as they understand them. Forsyth, from a modern reformed point of view, argued:

> . . . Clearly the two Baptisms, infant and adult, are psychologically different, though they have in common the main thing—the connection with the Word and its blessings in a faithful Church. In one case the experience precedes the act; in the other it follows (or it does not). . . . In adult baptism we are baptized *on* faith; in infant baptism *into* faith; but both are justified by faith only. [13]

There are three positions held among Baptists regarding baptism and church membership: (1) Some reject infant baptism as Christian baptism and restrict admission to the Lord's Table to those who have been baptized as believers. (2) Others likewise reject infant baptism but admit to the Lord's Table all who profess faith in Jesus Christ whether baptized as infants or as believers. (3) Still others say "Yes" and "No" to infant baptism. They admit to membership and to the

[12] A. Gilmore, *Baptism and Christian Unity* (Valley Forge: The Judson Press, 1966) pp. 10-16.

[13] P. T. Forsyth, *The Church and the Sacraments* (London: Independent Press, Ltd., 1955) p. 214.

Lord's Table any professed believers who have received only infant baptism without requiring re-baptism, but they practice only baptism of believers when receiving new converts.[14]

Gilmore feels that in this day when the ecumenical movement has drawn communions together and each acknowledges the others to be part of the one Holy Catholic Church, open membership is the only viable option for Christians who practice only believer's baptism. They ought, he believes, to recognize even a partial baptism or else quit saying that baptism does not matter. If, on the other hand, they insist on believer's baptism as an essential mark of the church, then they must be prepared to assert that the church did not exist for over a thousand years.[15]

Having recognized the need for reasonable concessions, the advocates of believer's baptism are faced by a dilemma in any plan of union with paedobaptists. Gilmore has stated it in this way:

> It is one thing to give partial recognition to infant baptism to the extent of requiring some form of baptism as a condition of membership and of acknowledging that other form when it has already taken place. It is a vastly different matter to refuse believers' baptism to an individual simply because their [sic] parents chose to have them baptized in infancy. . . . For one thing, it cuts right across the Baptist understanding of the freedom of the individual soul before God. . . . Moreover, it is felt by many Baptists that to accept such a situation would in fact yield the death blow to believers' baptism.[16]

This dilemma has presented itself in the formulation of a Plan of Church Union for North India and Pakistan and in the Consultation on Church Union in the United States. In the Plan for North India and Pakistan and in the Principles of Union adopted by the Consultation, the position has been

14 Gilmore, *op. cit.*, p. 62.
15 *Ibid.*, p. 81.
16 *Ibid.*, p. 75.

taken that there is only one baptism (with alternative practices of infant baptism and believer's baptism). It is therefore unrepeatable in the life of any one person, no matter by which method it was administered.

In the Plan for North India and Pakistan, the position is also taken that ministers should not seek to persuade people brought up with one form of baptism to adopt the alternative for themselves or their children. It is then stated that:

> . . . in the event of a person already baptized in infancy being led to the conviction that believers' baptism is more truly in keeping with the mind of Christ, "the ministers of the Church will help such a person to seek the remedy of what he now believes to be a grave lack in his own Baptism, not by re-baptism, but by some other means which effectively reaffirms his Baptism and symbolizes for him his engrafting into Christ. . . .
>
> "It is further understood that, if a person should persistently maintain that only his Baptism now as a believer will satisfy his conscience, although he was baptized in infancy, the minister concerned will refer the matter to the Bishop of the Diocese for pastoral advice and direction." [17]

Baptists, who have been participants in the formulation of this Plan for North India and Pakistan, have issued a Declaration of Principle of the Baptist Churches which they set forth in accepting the Constitution, and which is attached as an Appendix to that document. We record it here because it illustrates how one Free Church body has sought to overcome the difficulties which we have been discussing in this chapter:

> 1. That our Lord and Savior Jesus Christ, God manifest in the flesh, is the sole and absolute authority in all matters pertaining to faith and practice, as revealed in the Holy Scriptures, and that each Church has liberty, under the guidance of the Holy Spirit, to interpret and administer His laws.
>
> 2. That Christian baptism is the immersion in water into the Name of the Father, Son, and the Holy Ghost, of those who have professed repentance towards God and faith in our Lord Jesus Christ who

[17] *Ibid.,* p. 86.

"died for our sins according to the Scriptures; was buried and rose again the third day."

3. That it is the duty of every disciple to bear personal witness to the Gospel of Jesus Christ, and to take part in the evangelization of the world.

4. Baptist Churches in freely accepting the Constitution of the Church of North India/Pakistan take note that it allows for the Baptism of infants, which is a practice contrary to Baptist conviction, but they further take note that the provision is made for the dedication of infants and the administration of Baptism by immersion as the seal of conscious faith, and that profession of faith is required of those baptized in infancy before admission to membership in full standing in the Church, thereby acknowledging the nature of the Church as the fellowship of believers.

5. Baptist Churches again take note that the Constitution of the Church of North India/Pakistan in being episcopal involves some limitation on the freedom of the local Church, but they further take note that the episcopate is to be constitutional, with reasonable provision for all believers to share in seeking the mind of Christ in the affairs of the Church so far as they are able, and that the Church of North India/Pakistan acknowledges the Lordship of Christ in His Church.

6. Therefore Baptist Churches which, in fellowship with other Baptist Churches, have by due process after seeking the guidance of the Holy Spirit, decided to enter into the Church of North India/Pakistan, have acted in exercise of the liberty that they have always claimed, under the guidance of the Holy Spirit, to interpret and administer the Laws of Christ, believing that it is the will of God that they should be one with all who sincerely love the Lord Jesus Christ, recognizing the right of fellow-believers to certain practices which they themselves cannot commend, even as others recognize their freedom to follow the demands of conscience, and recognizing that Christian liberty is to be exercised in fellowship with other believers. In this they have sought, as Baptist Churches have always claimed to seek, the Lord's will as it has been made known unto them, or as it yet shall be made known.[18]

18 *Plan of Church Union in North India and Pakistan* (Rev. ed.; published by The Christian Literature Society, 1957), pp. 44-45. (Numerals have been inserted by the writer.)

The future of the Free Churches' participation in the growing movement towards more visible unity among Christians will depend in part, at least, upon their readiness to reassess the historic factors which brought them into existence and to determine what lasting contribution they can and should make to the larger church. Certainly, their stress upon the freedom of conscience in matters of religion, their emphasis upon the importance of the Scriptures as a guide to an understanding of God's will for all mankind, and their recognition of the subordination of structures to the life of the Spirit are contributions which can contribute greatly to the balance which should exist in the church between unity and diversity, structure and spiritual reality, and flexibility for mission and stability of witness. In a time when the fundamental ideals of the Free Church tradition are imperiled by a climate that is not congenial to the significance of the individual in society, the Free Churches would do well to preserve their contribution within the larger context of the whole Christian church rather than outside of it. In this direction lies the ultimate resolution of the dilemma of the Free Churches.

A SELECTED BIBLIOGRAPHY

Note: The reader may find in the footnotes information concerning sources not listed here. This list is intended to be helpful to the reader who desires to go beyond this book in his study of the subject.

Baptists and Unity. Published by Baptist Union of Great Britain and Ireland, 1966. 60 pp.

Blakemore, W. B., ed., *Renewal of the Church.* Three volumes. St. Louis: The Bethany Press, 1963. Contains the papers of a "Panel of Scholars" appointed to study the Disciple heritage in the light of the present situation.

Erickson, Claiborne R., *Baptists and Church Union in North India.* A Th.M. thesis in typescript, Berkeley Baptist Divinity School, Calif., 1967. viii, 189 pp.

Clark, H. W., *History of English Nonconformity.* Two volumes. London: Chapman and Hall, Limited, 1911.

Consultation on Church Union. Cincinnati: Forward Movement Publications, 1967. 144 pp.

Davies, Horton, *The English Free Churches.* New York: Oxford University Press, 1952. 208 pp.

DeGroot, Alfred T., *The Restoration Principle.* St. Louis: The Bethany Press, 1960. 191 pp.

Garrison, Winfred E., *Christian Unity and Disciples of Christ.* St. Louis: The Bethany Press, 1955. 286 pp.

──────, *The Quest and Character of a United Church.* Nashville: Abingdon Press, 1957. 238 pp.

Gilmore, A., *Baptism and Christian Unity.* Valley Forge: The Judson Press, 1966. 108 pp.

Grant, John W., *Free Churchmanship in England 1870-1940.* London: Independent Press, Ltd., n. d. vii, 424 pp.

Handy, Robert T., *Members One of Another.* Valley Forge: The Judson Press, 1959. 114 pp.

Horton, Douglas, *Toward an Undivided Church.* New York: Association Press and University of Notre Dame Press, 1967. 96 pp.

Jenkins, Daniel, *Congregationalism: A Restatement.* New York: Harper & Row, Publishers, 1954. 152 pp.

Jordan, W. K., *The Development of Religious Toleration in England.* Four volumes. Cambridge: Harvard University Press, 1932-1939.

Knapp, Forrest L., *Church Cooperation: Dead-End Street or Highway to Unity?* Garden City, N.Y.: Doubleday & Co., Inc., 1966. xi, 249 pp.

Latourette, Kenneth Scott, *The Emergence of a World Christian Community.* New Haven: Yale University Press, 1949. 91 pp.

Lecler, Joseph, S. J., *Toleration and the Reformation.* Translated from the French by T. L. Westow. Two volumes. New York: Association Press, 1960. 440, 532 pp.

Lee, Robert, *The Social Sources of Church Unity.* Nashville: Abingdon Press, 1960. 238 pp.

Littell, Franklin H., *The Free Church.* Boston: Starr King Press, 1957. xiii, 171 pp.

Loane, Marcus L., *Makers of Religious Freedom in the Seventeenth Century.* Two volumes. Grand Rapids: Wm. B. Eerdmans Publishing Co., 1961. 240 pp.

Marty, Martin E., *Church Unity and Church Mission.* Grand Rapids: Wm. B. Eerdmans Publishing Co., 1964. 139 pp.

Minear, Paul S., ed., *The Nature of the Unity We Seek.* St. Louis: The Bethany Press, 1958. 304 pp.

Osborn, Ronald E., *A Church for These Times.* Nashville: Abingdon Press, 1965. 192 pp.

Outler, Albert C., *The Christian Tradition and the Unity We Seek.* New York: Oxford University Press, Inc., 1957. xii, 165 pp.

Payne, Ernest A., *The Free Church Tradition in the Life of England.* Revised edition. London: Hodder & Stoughton Limited, 1965. 160 pp.

————, *The Free Churches and the State*. London: The Carey Kingsgate Press, Ltd., 1952. 29 pp.

————, *Free Churchmen, Unrepentant and Repentant*. London: The Carey Kingsgate Press, Ltd., 1965. 145 pp.

Piper, Otto A., *Protestantism in an Ecumenical Age*. Philadelphia: Fortress Press, 1965. ix, 254 pp.

Richardson, Cyril C., *The Church Through the Centuries*. New York: Charles Scribner's Sons, 1938. 255 pp.

Rouse, Ruth, and Neill, Stephen, eds., *A History of the Ecumenical Movement, 1517-1948*. Philadelphia: The Westminster Press, 1954. xxiv, 822 pp.

Routley, Erik, *English Religious Dissent*. Cambridge: University Press, 1960. 214 pp.

Scotford, John R., *Church Union: Why Not?* Boston: The Pilgrim Press, 1948. 123 pp.

Shakespeare, J. H., *The Churches at the Crossroads*. London: Williams and Norgate Press, 1918.

Shilitto, E., *The Hope and Mission of the Free Churches*. London: T. C. and E. C. Jack, 1913.

Simpson, E. P. Y., *Ordination and Christian Unity*. Valley Forge: The Judson Press, 1966. 184 pp.

Skeats, Herbert S., and Miall, Charles S., *History of the Free Churches of England, 1688-1891*. London: Alexander & Shepheard, 1891. xxiv, 757 pp.

Smith, H. Shelton, *et al.*, *American Christianity: An Historical Interpretation with Representative Documents*. Two volumes. New York: Charles Scribner's Sons, 1960, 1963.

Townsend, Henry, *The Claims of the Free Churches*. London: Hodder and Stoughton Limited, 1949. 320 pp.

Troeltsch, Ernest, *The Social Teachings of the Christian Churches*. Two volumes. New York: The Macmillan Company, 1949. 1019 pp.

Walton, Robert C., *The Gathered Community*. London: The Carey Kingsgate Press, Ltd., 1946. 184 pp.

Westin, Gunnar, *The Free Church Through the Ages*. Trans. by Virgil A. Olson. Nashville: The Broadman Press, 1958. x, 380 pp.

Wilkinson, John T., *1662 . . . and After: Three Centuries of English Nonconformity*. London: The Epworth Press, 1962. xiv, 269 pp.

Williams, George H., *The Radical Reformation*. Philadelphia: The Westminster Press, 1962. xxxi, 924 pp.

INDEX